TUESDAY NIGHT IN GRIMSBY
DIARY OF A MASOCHIST

Barrie Stradling

A Terrace Banter publication

Tuesday Night In Grimsby - Diary Of A Masochist (Pbk)

© Barrie Stradling, 2000

ISBN 0 9535920 5 7

Published by Terrace Banter, Scotland
Printed by Heritage Press, England

A Terrace Banter publication from
S.T. Publishing
P.O. Box 12, Lockerbie, Dumfriesshire. DG11 3BW. Scotland.
www.terracebanter.com

TUESDAY NIGHT IN GRIMSBY
DIARY OF A MASOCHIST

CHAPTER 1

THE BELEAGUERED FORTRESS

I WAS BORN in Stepney in London's East End, the wrong side of the river according to many. Nowadays this wouldn't be considered a catchment area for Millwall, but the club was still seen as an East End team by many people on our side of the river in the late 1950s and although my father supported Tottenham, my cousin, uncle, and three next door neighbours all supported Millwall.

The first game I was ever taken to was in 1965 when my Dad took me to West Ham to see Stanley Matthews play. The game ended 3-3. I suppose it must have been one of Stan's last games.

My next game and my first visit to my true spiritual home was on the 29th of August, 1966, to see the Lions play Brentford in a League Cup replay. All I can recall about the game was that Brentford's goalkeeper wore white gloves, Millwall lost 1-0, and Millwall's forward, Joe Broadfoot, missed from about a foot out, an omen of things to come if ever I've seen one.

Once bitten by the football bug, I used to go practically every week, to Tottenham with my Dad one week and to Millwall with my cousin Roy the next week. The good thing about watching Tottenham at this time was that I got to see many players who've since become legends - Best, Charlton, Law, Moore, Banks and Jimmy Greaves (a great player, but a bit of a prat as a pundit).

Even at this time, it became apparent to me that The Den wasn't like other grounds, particularly in comparison to Tottenham. I found Spurs fans very quick to get on their team's backs, but Millwall seemed to get behind their team much more, particularly in adversity. This admirable trait seems to have been lost somewhat in the recent years, where it isn't uncommon for Millwall players and the team in general to get as much, if not more, abuse than the opposition. Perhaps it's the old adage about nostalgia not being what it used to be, but I'm sure that this facet of Millwallism is a recent phenomenon.

However, there was, and to a degree still is, no place like The Den, a place where opposition players and fans alike dread going. It once prompted a quote from Joe Royle, when manager of Oldham, that he'd "rather be a rear gunner in the Lebanon than a linesman at

Millwall". Quite what sort of "rear gunner" he is referring to, I'll leave open for your interpretation.

This sort of comment is music to my ears. Who wants an opposing team enjoying a game at your ground? The Den: loud, passionate, loyal, hostile, and not to say violent. What more could a young working class inner city kid want?

The Old Den wasn't what you'd call salubrious, but we called it home. The toilet facilities for example were a real treat and left just a bit to be desired. For example, a ladies toilet was somewhat of a rare commodity, the attitude being "football's a man's game, love, try New Cross Gate station". I think there was a loo, but as I'm a chap, I never ventured there, even in an emergency. The men's facilities weren't much better - not so much "Now wash your hands" as "I'd recommend a tetanus jab, sir". At the Cold Blow Lane, the main toilet consisted of a wall open to the skies, very down to nature and all that, allowing for God's natural cleaner, rain, to wash out periodically. It was a place where any shyness you had would go out of the window. Man and boy, we stood together without a hint of a modesty barrier or any of that nonsense. Very cosy, uninhibiting and hygenic it was too. Now I've put you off your tea I'll move on . . .

Something I never saw at any other ground was the bi-weekly fans versus police tugs of war which took place, as the police snatch squads would attempt to drag some supposed perpetrator over the pitch wall, pre-Colditz fence. They would be met with The Den crowd pulling an arm or leg in an attempt to drag one of their own back into the crowd and away from the long arm of the law. A competition that usually ended in a Millwall victory with the police's victim vanishing back into the throng. This happened mostly in the late 60s and 70s and was always an amusing sight. Well I thought so anyway.

To say that watching football at Millwall over the years has been an experience would be a massive understatement. I think it covers every event it is possible to witness at a football ground, European glory nights excepted.

The Old Den was unique in my experience at the time. I'd been to Upton Park, White Hart Lane, The Valley, Highbury and Stamford Bridge, but to my mind nothing compared to the hot bed that was Millwall in the late 60s and early 70s. The ground before the days of crowd segregation days was a fantastically noisy place. A scientific study was done at the time that showed The Den was noisier than Anfield with far less people, so it must be true.

6

The usual form for home games was to stand behind the end Millwall were attacking. This usually meant that the Cold Blow Lane end of the ground was sardine like in the second half, when the more Romany-like supporters would join us in swelling the numbers to roar The Lions on. It was said in the old days that the crowd was worth a goal start. The constant noise, the squalid surroundings and the open hostility certainly went a long way to assisting Millwall to set up an unbeaten home run of 59 games, a record at the time.

To me it was this passion, not to say partisan hostility, that stays with you for life. It tends to be the glue which holds the foundations of a lifetime affiliation together.

Over the years, I've been caged behind barriers and fences at The Old Den that would give the camp on Blood Island a run for its money. I've been to night matches that were more like cock fights or bear pits than football matches, the surrounding darkness just adding to the usual air of menace, all played out in the early days against the surreal backdrop of the New Cross dog track floodlights, the broken clocks, and the freeloading masses on Jews Hill.

I was lucky enough to see the tail-end of the unbeaten run, including its culmination against Plymouth and I've seen and heard many hostile night games, but the sheer intensity of the League Cup second leg game against Chelsea in October, 1984, was the most volatile I can recall. As you can imagine, this was up against some pretty stiff competition.

It pleases me to think that The New Den is now coming close to The Old Den for atmosphere, with the CBL and East Stand mimicking the old CBL and Halfway Line combination in years gone by, particularly noticeable for recent games against Cardiff, Man. City, Bristol City, and for Birmingham's last visit. This, as they almost say, "suits me sir".

The things I've seen at home over the last 30 years are certainly wide and varied, as I hope the following goes some way to expressing. So in no particular order . . .

I've seen pitch invasions, including a referee, Norman Burtinshaw, supposedly attacked in a game against Aston Villa. I've seen Derby players "attacked" during the second leg of the play-off debacle. I've seen Pressman of Sheffield Wednesday, Brevett of Fulham, and the ever lovely Stan Collymore confronted by fans, the latter also being substituted in a friendly for Liverpool for his usual antics before the referee sent him off. I've seen a former Millwall player, Paul Roberts, getting lippy with the CBL after a goal for his new club, Brentford, only for a fan to calmly climb over the Stalag defences and cease his celebrations with a soothing fist, much to the home fans obvious delight.

I've seen away goalkeepers stand as far away from the home fans as common sense would allow to avoid the barracking. I've seen teams visit The Old Den in particular, and visibly wilt under the relentless volume and hostility. I've seen opposition teams pelted with coins, particularly West Ham in the "old" First Division, only for their captain, Alvin Martin, to say he wished West Ham fans were as passionate as us.

I've seen Nigel Winterburn felled by a coin against Arsenal in a League Cup game in the 90s, an Olympic throwing champion in the making here I think. I've seen the less than well thought out blanket collections that used to go around The Den in the 60s and 70s, where people were encouraged to fill blankets with coins from the terraces for charity - surprisingly the outcome was the blanket carriers became the main target and got pelted.

I've seen surgical masks, Scottish flags, a big bass drum, I've been to mid-week afternoon games during the three day week power cuts, I've seen missile throwing, smoke bombs against Portsmouth, the first ever game played on a Sunday v Fulham.

I've seen the flags, etc., against Blackburn Rovers in 1988 that celebrated our crowning as Division Two (old) Champions and made The Den look like a scene from Gazzetta Italia. I've seen Derby County win the Division Two Championship at our ground dressed in our away shirts in 1969. I've seen Brian Clough given a standing ovation from tunnel to dug out in his Notts Forest days in Division One. I've seen a sadly premature wild pitch celebration to confirm our promotion to Division One in 1972 - we finished third when the next season a rule change would have meant automatic promotion.

I've seen The Old Den dismantled and the sacred turf thrown around and towards the directors in a final act of defiance against our forced exodus. I've seen away fans "run" on a regular basis, I've seen an ill advised attempt by Swansea fans to "take" the Cold Blow Lane end in the 1980s which was met with all the ferocity an Englishman could muster in defending his castle, where young and old joined the fray to expel the intruders until the police led the battered invaders to on pitch safety - The Den remained untaken to the end.

I've seen the club go through more ground closures and FA sanctions than any other club. I've seen Millwall install the first crèche for a football ground and introduce, I believe, the first "care for the local community" scheme - not "care in the community" as our media image would have you believe. I've seen the club go to the wall, no pun intended, and come back from imminent extinction.

I've seen big crowds - 31,000 v Leicester in an FA Cup tie in 1969 - and seasons when we've rattled around The Den during the dark days under Petchey, Anderson, and even George Graham, to minuscule crowds. I've seen "riots" inside and outside both incarnations of The Den, I've seen great wins and terrible defeats, great comebacks (Sheffield Wednesday 4-2!) and capitulations.

A pretty chequered history, I'm sure you'll agree. Some things like the crèche and local community schemes are not publicity worthy according to our sensation seeking national media. If I'm truthful, there have probably been more lows than highs in terms of playing success during the 30 odd years I've supported The Lions, but I have seen Millwall play two seasons in the top Division and play at Wembley, albeit in the Auto Windscreen Trophy Final. But for a supporter of what is generally considered to be a lesser side to London's elite, and a pariah to the rest of football, these are a fulfilment of my football life dreams. Anything else is a bonus, as they say.

I'm sure all football fans can quote incidents that make their teams special to them, but none compares to the soap opera that is Millwall. In brief, who can boast a record unbeaten home League record (at the time), more ground closures and FA sanctions than any other, more derogatory column inches than Jack The Ripper would have got, a more passionate crowd than any other club (who it's true have committed many crimes in the name of this passion), a decibel record for crowd noise, riots, pitch invasions, oh, and football matches, financial administration and a Chairman in the 60s who would have been better served having an emergency glass repair shop than a car lot? And last, and possibly least, the first purpose built (white elephant) ground post Taylor report, a construction that's proved to be more of a millstone than a milestone?

Anyway, enough of this, time to leave home.

CHAPTER 2

MY EXCUSE ANYWAY

FOR ANYONE INTERESTED in astrology, I'm a Leo, a lion in astrological and football affinity terms. However, I've yet to find a personality trait attributable to my star sign that mentions masochism as a characteristic, but it's obviously a facet of my make up, because I am, for my sins, a long suffering away traveller. Any uninitiated family style, floating supporter whose idea of supporting their team is to wear their club shirt and bobble hat sitting in front of Sky Sport will probably read the following book and feel I definitely need my head examined.

But for a seasoned away traveller, the grief suffered is one of the disease symptoms you have to endure to follow your team the length and breadth of the country. It is made particularly poignant by the fact that I follow a team who've under-achieved massively over the years, winning few trophies or in truth, few friends, in their history.

Before my own adventures began, travelling away required a tenacity and determination of Stanley and Livingstone proportions in the days prior to a motorway network and when the rail system was just one step up from Stephenson's Rocket. To venture anywhere up north would sometimes take days, if you arrived at all. The older fans I've spoken to talk of the true pioneer spirit of it all. For example one of my regular home and away companions, Dave, who's about ten years older than me, tells of a time when on a trip to Carlisle. The train got stuck in a blizzard and in a scene more akin to *Dr Zhivago* than a football match, the passengers had to sleep on the train until "International Rescue" came and dug them out. This sort of devotion to duty puts even my exploits in the shade and makes me look like a lightweight fair weather Charlie. My hat goes off to you!

The only alternative in the 60s and 70s was the vague possibility of Millwall appearing on *Match Of The Day* or *The Big Match*. At this time there was a requirement to show a certasin number of lower league games, so you might, if you were lucky, see a fuzzy black and white (or if posh, colour) snippet of the action featuring Millwall at some far flung forgotten northern corner of the Empire. Even a small snatch, if you'll pardon the expression, was better than no snatch at all, a sentiment I'm sure you'll all share.

Nowadays the media seems utterly obsessed with the Premiership and totally ignores the quarter of a million First to Third Division regulars. Sky is much better than terrestrial TV, where the only Nationwide League highlights are shown in the middle of the night and even then only the goals. Very shortsighted, I'd say.

A programme that did highlight the differences between earlier away travel and today's draconian measures was the infamous *Panorama* documentary. Although more famous for its violent content, it did show Millwall fans travelling on a coach with what looked like no alcohol or cigarette restrictions, and with very little segregation or police interference. Nothing to stop the "steaming" and "offs". Much more like a jolly boys beano than today's Big Brother style. Nowadays it's much, much more restrictive with "dry" trains and coaches, no alcohol, no smoking, no waccy baccy, just enjoy yourself.

I've been on many away coaches which have been methodically searched in a Popeye Doyle looking for heroin in *The French Connection* stylee. Heaven forbid anyone smuggling a light ale on board, it's *Midnight Express* for you my lad! On arrival it's usually mass policing and segregation and overly enthusiastic (in some instances) stewards giving you a full body search. Sometimes lady stewards are there for this task. These, for some reason, don't seem to cause the same resentment as a fellow man searching you. In fact queues can form for this vicarious thrill, and why not? One tip to piss off the more nosey stewards is to wear something like a fishing coat with about 50 pockets. That'll serve the buggers right.

I suppose it is safer nowadays, but I do wonder what sort of response you would get if you treated the crowd at the Royal Opera House as they do a football crowd, say, having to take their pearls off in case they used them as a weapon, passing through metal detectors, etc., and being man handled in a manner Diana Ross wouldn't take kindly to. I'm sure if Lord Snooty and his ilk were on the receiving end it would be stopped quick sharp.

The true away traveller has to withstand more hardships than Ranulph Fiennes would sensibly endure. It's not a pre-occupation taken up lightly; it's a path to madness, bettered only by 92 league ground collectors, the sort of people who will go to a ground just to add it to the list – very fulfilling I'm sure. In my mind I can justify following my team to the ends of the Earth, or Burnley as it's known, but the concept of going all moist at the thought of a Halifax v. Cheltenham clash on a wet Wednesday in December seems perverse even to my masochistic leanings.

To date I've visited 79 different clubs, and I've also been to two Dens, two Walsalls, two Stokes, two Wigans, two Readings, three Bristol Rovers and two Brighton incarnations. All to watch my beloved Lions, and these visits covering the top three Divisions only. Thankfully I've not had the pleasure of Division Three (Four), as I was fortunately too young. If I were to develop "ground hopititus", I would have to hope Millwall get relegated or go on a long Cup run against the "stiffs", either of which pleasures I can forego I'm sure.

I was prompted to write a book about my away travel adventures after reading *Fever Pitch* by Nick Hornby, and whilst it's an excellent book and film, a couple of things struck me. My Dad wasn't Neil Pearson and didn't have a snazzy car coat, and if that is fever I must be on my last legs with malaria.

As a love story / fan history it works well, but is a universe away from following a team who've table hopped and only tasted moderate success. Women's FA Cup, Football League trophy, a couple of FA Youth Cups, and London five-a-sides - oh! and a couple of Division Championships and FA Cup semi finals - in their history.

Following Millwall home and away (cue theme tune!) has meant developing a thick skin to match my intellect. You're treated like a pariah or an invading army wherever you go, you'll be penned in, made to play games on Sunday mornings to avoid trouble, video-taped at every given opportunity ("I'm ready for my close-up, Mr Constable!") and treated like the scum of the Earth all over the country. Not true in the main, contrary to media image, but positive images do not a sensation make and thus don't flog papers.

In *Fever Pitch*, Arsenal play at Anfield in an (old) Division One decider. I watched it on TV (but I don't support Arsenal), and so does Nick Hornby. Now if Millwall were in contention for any league, let alone the Premiership, I'd walk there and pay whatever it took to acquire a ticket. Just ask my mates, they'd tell you – go on, ask them!

In fact, I've only watched three Millwall games live / videoed on TV, where it's been impossible for me to go for one reason or another. To add authenticity, I search myself and have sound effect tapes of police sirens and helicopter noises playing to make it more true to life. Also for these games, I've found myself standing up in the living room to watch the TV, not the act of a rational man, I'm sure you'll agree.

In this book, I've tried to give you a feel for what it's like to be an away traveller, with Millwall in my case. All I've witnessed or done over the years. I've tried to cover the rich tapestry of experiences from the absurd, to the funny, to the violent. Well, it is Millwall – it would be rude not to include it.

All that follows is true, armchair fans, believe it or not.

CHAPTER 3

YOU COULDN'T MAKE IT UP

AS AN INTREPID away traveller and veteran of 250 plus away games, I've seen some bizarre things on my travels. I thought I'd let you into my world. I don't think you could experience such "Mr Bean" moments sitting securely on your sofa glued to the Sunday or Monday Sky Football broadcasts somehow. For example . . .

We went to Wycombe a couple of seasons ago and were treated to a floodlight failure, a sprinkler with a mind of its own going beserk when the lights came back on, pre-match "entertainment" consisting of a brass band and a pyramid of acrobats - which David Sinclair, a Millwall player (sic) at the time, kept kicking balls at, a 1-0 defeat, and the dubious pleasure of a home fan mooning and flashing his knob at us from on top of a station bound bus. Beat that, Richard Keys.

At a night match in Macclesfield, we saw the refreshment staff cook enough food for ten times the amount of away fans. Perhaps they had a sub-contract with Glastonbury Festival? We stood on a freezing cold open terrace to witness a 2-0 win on a swamp of a pitch and gazed upon the splendour that is the Moss Rose ground. Let me describe it to you. Our end, an open to the elements terrace, to my left a "stand" taking up about a third of the side with a bit of terracing, the opposite "home end" consisting of about 12 steps of terracing and another "stand" of about six rows of seats, and last but not least, to my right, a structure that looked like they had lifted it lock, stock and barrel from The Raj. It had a green and white striped roof arrangement over a small amount of seating. If you had seen the Brigadier and his good lady wife emerge after a spot of tiffin, you wouldn't have been at all surprised. Very *It Ain't Half Hot Mum!*, I'm sure, except for the shorts, Windsor Davies, and the heat obviously! Old Trafford it ain't.

I've been taken to a pub by the police in Blackburn, and by our coach driver to a snooker club in Sunderland. Jolly good idea, I thought, half cut and possibly having to fight your way out. Well done! For an altogether more masochistic 6-0 defeat at Roker Park, I've stood next to t-shirted locals in temperatures that would make huskies head back under the duvet.

I've fallen arse over tip outside Barnsley station whilst running to catch our special home and not noticing an ideally positioned bollard which was on an un-lit concourse. Not too disasterous, you may think. Well no, but unfortunately I had a plastic bottle full of real orange juice in my pocket, so for a good two hour ride I was covered in grit and mud from my fall and soaked in said orange juice. I spent the journey ringing my coat out and picking handfuls of "pith" from my pocket, trying to salvage what was in the pocket with the bottle. On arrival at Kings Cross / St Pancras, my attempts to get a cab home were somewhat hindered by my general appearance being a cross between a West End beggar and someone who would be considered too scruffy to sell *The Big Issue*. I did get a cab, but I kept waiting for him to drop me off at the nearest soup kitchen.

Prior to rebuilding, Notts County's ground was a bit grim, to say the least. My mate Micky and I were greeted by the following sight – an old rusty round-arched shed on one side, at the opposite end a 40 foot high brick wall, and a more normal if decrepit stand on the other side. We stood on a dilapidated open terrace surrounded by Colditz style fencing. To add to the flavour of the day, it was horribly grey and overcast, the home team emerged in a colourful black and white strip, and *Robin Hood* by Dick James echoed around the ground. At this point, Micky said "If we lose here, I'm going to top myself", so drab and depressing was it. Thankfully we won 1-0 and The Samaritans were spared the task of talking Micky down from a bridge over the Trent.

On another trip to Notts County, this time to a vastly improved Meadow Lane (so much so that I honestly thought I was at the wrong ground), the 40 foot wall now made sense as a perch for the executive boxes, but the strange creatures depicted in the seats took a bit of deciphering. My companion this time being another mate, Simon, I turned to him before the match and said, "Who's that fat cunt running around the pitch?", as in my considered medical opinion, he should sit down before he pegged out. We didn't have the answer until the officials came out for the kick-off and this fine figure of a man was in fact the referee.

On a similar note at yet another visit to the same ground, County's keeper Steve Cherry was greeted with chants of "Blobby, Blobby, Blobby" each time he had the misfortune to touch the ball. I'm sure he's eternally grateful to Noel Edmonds for this one. And for yet another trip to Notts County the PA announcer had whistling dentures, with every "s" sounding like a kettle boiling! Marvellous.

Once again in Nottingham, this time at Forest for a mid-week League Cup game, which we amazingly won, in an act of unfortunate timing, a bloke sitting close to me and Simon arrived back at his seat with a cardboard tray of full, boiling hot drinks, just as Greg Berry scored. The obvious dilemma being "Do I react normally and throw my hands up in the air?", thus scalding all and sundry, or "Have an inward celebration until I can put the tray down?" Fortunately for us he decided the latter. It's enough of a shock seeing us win, let alone having to have plastic surgery into the bargain.

Simon, myself, and another mate called Mick, went to Sheffield United for a 1-1 game in the 1990s. At this time the stand to the left of the away fans had been demolished, awaiting reconstruction. This left one side totally open to the elements. It was on this day that a criminal mastermind chose to break into a house opposite the ground, a burglary carried out in full view of the whole crowd. Leading to its natural conclusion, we'd have a *Guinness Book Of Records* 10,000 strong identity parade, with a queue around the block to say, "That's him!"

At Gillingham in 1999, Millwall's young striker Richard Sadlier was listed in the programme as being 12 foot three inches tall. No wonder he usually doesn't bother to jump.

A visit to Peterborough, by train brings you into contact with Pets World on the way to the ground. This always make me think of tortoises and alsations etc., with bar codes on them for scanning. Picture the scene – a till attendant holding aloft a rottweiler to ask "How much is this Sharon? The bar code won't work!" Nothing to do with football, I'm afraid, just the workings of a warped mind.

At a game at Eastville in 1984, another "San Siroesque" ground, for a 1-1 draw against Bristol Rovers, it was so cold on the open end that we built a small fire on the terrace around which some of the crowd danced Red Indian style, singing "E-I-O, E-I-O", the origin of that strange chant you may have heard at The Den. Also at this game we were abused by passing traffic from the flyover behind and above us, and at the end the police pinned us in an alleyway behind the terrace with horses. Just an average day out!

I went to Coventry in our second season in Division One. At this time we were in freefall under the stewardship of Uncle Bob "Comfy Cardie" Pearson. We scored first, but lost 3-1. This game was played out under a cloud that not only looked like the end of the world, but rained like it as well. It was at this game that I found the appropriately titled book, *Misery*, under the seat. Not only was this fortunate in that I didn't have it and I used to read Stephen King books at the time, but its title being so apt was a bit spooky.

At a night match in Crewe, I met a friend of my mate, Dave, who'd come over from Ireland for the match and endured a ferry breakdown on the way there. I couldn't help feeling envious as I only needed this travelling disaster to complete the set, as you will see in the following chapters.

For a game at Preston in the 1990s, we were greeted by the sight of a huge depiction of Tom Finney's head on the new stand opposite us. Very nice it was too, but I couldn't help thinking of a likely conversation at the ticket office - "It's almost sold out, you'll have to sit on Tom Finney's face I'm afraid!" At this game, which we lost, their was a junior Wild West punch-up outside, which ended up in a nearby garden.

Just a note to point out, if you go to Grimsby (Cleethorpes, Eeh! The glamour of it all), it stinks of fish miles before you arrive, the seats on the away end are so close together that you're locked in like stocks and your knees are under your chin, and there's no atmosphere, particularly from the aptly named Findus Stand. Just thought you'd like to know.

Some games are a catalogue of disasters. One game at Stoke City, which we lost 3-2, I think, in the 1990s was one such. Stoke scored a late winner, the club coach took an age to get back, and when I did eventually arrive home, I found that my cable TV box didn't work and nor did my mobile. So I went to a local phone box, which amazingly hadn't been wrecked, and rang the cable company, only to find that their repairs engineers didn't work again until Monday. Then unbeknown to me, on my return to my flat I'd trod in a load of dog shit, which I managed to tread into my new beige carpet. The perfect end to a perfect day.

My only visit to Lincoln, so far, came a week after the mad house of Maine Road, and more of a contrast it would be hard to envisage. Simon and I went up on a club coach which arrived early, so we pulled into a nearby country pub. We told the bar staff who we were and I'm sure they feared the worst. Nothing of the sort, we had a pleasant couple of pints and left for the ground to be met by home fans letting off balloons, singing jolly songs and all to the backbeat of a brass band. We lost 2-0 on a pitch like a sandy beach. Man City it wasn't.

My only game at an amateur ground came at Dagenham (or "Nam" as the locals call it) for a much postponed FA Cup game in 1981. We won 2-0, I stood on a grassy verge in the freezing cold behind the goal, on Essex boy "wedge haircut" alert. We also occupied a side stand to my left, and when Millwall scored the people in this stand surged forward, the hastily constructed advertising hoarding / wall collapsing beneath them.

We went to Middlesbrough when Bruce Rioch was our manager. Dear old Brucie, "Good game, good game?" No, not really Bruce! He'd been 'Boro's manager when they almost went out of business, saved them, and came back to a prodigal son / fatted calf style welcome. He'd practically bought a new team for this beginning of season game, after our previous season's play-off failure. We scanned the pitch, didn't recognise anyone, and so we beckoned the nearest Millwall player over. "Who are you?"

"Chris Armstrong," came the reply.

The conversation then went something like, "Who's he? Who? Well who's he then? Really! Well, who's he then?" You get the picture.

In the 70s, Millwall had two of the earlier batch of black players, Trevor Lee and Phil Walker. Both good players and crowd favourites, as is often the case at racist or supposedly racist clubs, the same applying to John Fashanu and Tony Witter in more recent times. Of the two, Trevor Lee was the more interesting because he had the full blown *Blaxploitation* afro hairdo. One of his main attributes, home or away, was the back flick at the near post from corners. This was an effective ploy, which you don't seem to see as much nowadays. Perhaps I'm just not looking. I think an opportunity was missed, however, and a more ingenious tactic could have been employed. I'll run it by you, tell me what you think.

Gordon Hill or whoever could float the corner in to the near post, Trevor could rise and let the ball burrow into his afro, thus confusing the defenders who would be left scratching their chins, etc, as he calmly walked across the line with the ball firmly attached to the old busby and wait for the ref to confirm the goal once he was able to dislodge the ball. A fiendish ploy, what do you think? Perhaps I'm just talking nonsense. Believe me, it wouldn't be the first (or last) time.

Football inflatables, what the hell was that about? In the very old days the only inflatable you might see was a Zeppelin, but in the 80s and early 90s this strange phenomenon arose.

"I'm off to football, dear."

"Okay, but don't forget your six foot banana."

Weird.

I remember the shoal of herrings, if that's the phrase, which Grimsby displayed at Wimbledon for a Cup game. They should have brought real fish, the benefits being two-fold. One, it would have made them feel at home, and two, it would have guaranteed every one of them an unaccompanied seat on the bus.

This sort of thing never seems to catch on at Millwall. I suppose we're too sophisticated and cool being Londoners. Naturally the club did try to flog an inflatable rampant lion at The Old Den, which went down like a lead balloon and to my recollection only lasted one game. That aside, being Millwall we obviously had to endure the hilarious press cartoon showing a skinhead with a Stanley knife with "Millwall" written along it. Very droll and naturally not a cheap shot at all. Oh no!

My mate, Steve Kimberley, and I went to Southend United for my first visit there, on a Monday night in September, 1983. It pissed down all night and we sought shelter on the terrace beneath the home stand. We lost 3-2, and after the game we decided to find a pub to drown our sorrows. As we didn't know the area too well and, as usual, most places were shut for our visit anyway, we drove around in Steve's car and found a pub some way off the beaten track, got inside, ordered our drinks and then took a look around the pub, as you do. It began to dawn on us that all was not as it should be. All the men in the bar appeared to be couples and there wasn't a woman in sight. It was a gay bar - eek! We drank up, made our excuses and left. All a horrible mistake, honest.

Another similar incident happened again accidentally, I can assure you. This time with another mate, Steve Fisher, an East End Millwall fan like myself. I'd arranged to meet him for a drink in Mile End and took a short cut through a park which houses the grandiosely named East London Stadium. On the outer edge of this park there was a pub that I believe was originally called Inn On The Park. In the 80s it had been a disco type pub playing soul and dance music. It had been closed for a while, but had been a regular watering hole for us all prior to this.

As I got closer I could smell a barbeque on the go at the rear of the pub and the strains of Johnny Cash singing *Burning Ring Of Fire* echoing across the park. I met up with Steve and said that I'd just passed the pub by the park and it was open. We decided to try it out and passed the bouncer on the door not suspecting anything. However once inside the full horror dawned. What we'd walked into was like a Freddie Mercury lookalike contest, full of men in satin shorts, with bushy Merv Hughes style moustaches, and leather gear without a motorbike in sight. Oops! Steve said "Sod it! We're here now, let's have a drink anyway." So we did and he tried to chat the barmaid up, who surprisingly turned out to be a lesbian. Still if you don't ask, you don't know, do you? Again we made our excuses and left.

This reminds me of Brighton's visit to The Old Den in the early 90s when they turned up resplendent in a red and white thinly striped shirt that looked pink from a distance and had the name of their sponsor, Nobo, proudly displayed on their chests. Someone's idea of a joke or an honest attempt to show what Brighton's renowned or infamous for? Who knows.

At Bournemouth during the 1999 / 2000 season, we came out of the station and headed towards the ground past XXX video shops in the town's answer to Soho. We got back to the station before it got dark so we didn't get the full sordid delight of it all. However, a couple of times when I've had a closer look at such things, though not football related, were in Paris and New York. In Paris, five of us went over to see the British Lions play France in a celebration match for the French R.F.U. In the afternoon prior to the game we had a wander around trying to find the Moulin Rouge so we could book it up for after the match. On the way we ended up in the red light / live sex show area. The bloke on one of the doors trying to drum up custom looked at us, saw that we didn't have berets on and didn't have a string of onions, so assumed we were English. "Ah! Roast beef, live sex inside, Maggie Thatcher, sucky fucky donkey!"

My God, what a thought! The old patter needs a bit of work, mate! Needless to say we weren't tempted and only just managed to keep our dinner down at the image he'd put in our heads.

In the early 90s I went for a short five day break to New York, arrived on a Friday night, went out for a drink and due to jet lag, got up early on Saturday morning and wandered down towards their Chelsea and SoHo. This was at about 9.00am. We passed a scene straight out of *Miami Vice* with toms and pimps hanging about looking for punters. One girl with peroxide blonde and hardly any clothes on got into a punter's car and drove away. We wandered around with no particular direction in mind when we came upon the same car parked up, with the same blonde head bobbing up and down. I think you know what I mean. A good old down home Yankee welcome to New York. Moral majority, yeah right!

In early 1991 we played at West Brom. At this time the Hawthorns was being refurbished and the away end was now like a building site. We were therefore crammed into a pokey side stand, crushed in like a tin of John West's sardines, when the home fans launched into the immortal "Is that all you take away?"

"Sorry, it was all we could get in the tin!"

Each time I hear this chant, I want to reply, "No, there's another 2,000 outside who didn't come in just to wind you up!" It's a very silly chant if you ask me. We sing it as well, but that obviously doesn't make it any more sensible.

Matthew Lorenzo, star of Sky Sport and former sports johnny on Thames / Carlton / LWT, and son of Peter Lorenzo, the commentator from the 60s and 70s on *Star Soccer* (blimey, that's a lot to live up to!), was working when we played a night match at Luton, if you can call it working. He very foolishly decided the best place for his pitch-side spiel was very close to the away stand. Good choice. Naturally he was abused, ridiculed and lambasted mercilessly. Even he must have realised this wasn't such a good idea. Still, serves him right for being a self-confessed Happy Hammer. He wasn't very happy that night though. Funny that.

Millwall suffered a rapid and spectacular plummet from the dizzy heights of leading the old First Division (twice) to dwellers of the netherworld of the new Division Two and all with indecent haste in a few short years. Some might say it was lack of talent, a string of hapless managers, a lack of financial backing or the simple fact that the incumbent players didn't try and did the old "Sod this, I'm off" routine the very instant that we'd been confirmed as down, but I have my own idea about why, and here it is:

Too many players in our recent past have not had manly names. Not so much "Tom, Dick and Harry" nowadays as "Quentin, Tarquin and Farquar" and the like. For example, Millwall have had, or still have, players called Kasey, Scott, Dean, Jason, Jamie and Warren. To me these sound more like a new boy band or a crack team of hairdressers than a top notch football outfit. Unfortunately during the Nineties, Millwall played more like the works team of Stanley Of Paris (Mile End Road), coiffeurists to the stars and syrup specialists, than a pro-team.

To add weight to my theory, I thought I'd run through the possible origins of where some people's names come from. Here goes:

Warren: As in Patmore, golfer extra-ordinaire. Probably named after Warren (Alf Garnett) Mitchell, rather than old "have knob will travel" Warren Beatty. Mind you, his only appearance was spare prick like, so who knows?

Scott: As in Fitzgerald. Probably named after Thunderbird's Scott Tracy. This is very apt considering the need for International Rescue's help at many of our frequent defensive disasters in the last decade. Or maybe after F Scott Fitzgerald, how posh.

Kasey: As in Keller. Probably named after Casey (Kasey?) Jones who used to wear a bizarre striped hat and a uniform like an oversized Andy Pandy (younger readers ask your parents!) He was renowned in song for "steaming" and "rolling". Sounds a bit violent to me.

Jason: As in Van Blerk, which sounds like a Geordie name for a "white van man", as in "This is Jason, he's that van blerk". Christian name unfortunately probably comes from cottager (and Fulham fan?), Peter (Jason King) Wyngarde. Trust me this is no recommendation, I can assure you.

Dean: As in Neal, White or Horrix. Slightly older players, but probably named after Dean Martin, a renowned old soak and naturally a great role model for any professional sportsman.

Jamie: As in Moralee. Probably named after fabulously breasted scream queen, Jamie Lee Curtis, and is more suited to her than a peroxide obsessed modern footballer.

To my mind, add a few more Burts, Harrys, Stans and the like, and our fortunes will immediately change for the better. You mark my words, it's true I tell you! For information, Millwall used to have a player called Jack Cock. Now that is a real man's name.

Millwall played at Gillingham in 1998 on a cold night in late December. In a bad tempered game, the most interesting thing about the night was self-confessed Millwall fan and Gills Chairman, Paul Scally, who in an act of media manipulation not bettered in the self promotion stakes by even Murdoch or Maxwell, managed to get his mugshot in the club programme no less than five times. Still it's his money I suppose.

At Southend in January, 1998, the true schizophrenic nature of a football crowd was beautifully displayed. At the time Southend had a slightly more filled out Neville Southall in goal for them and in his approach towards the away fans was greeted in equal measure with reverential applause in recognition of his excellent career and chants of "You fat bastard!" and "Who ate all the sheep?" in recognition of his newly acquired pie eating ability.

For a night match at Elm Park, Reading, in the 90s, which we won 2-1 and Uwe Fuchs made his debut, we were treated to ten minutes injury time, my first personal encounter with the modern phenomenon of "International Fergie Time", a time zone where it is required, whenever possible, to play on until the home team score. Unfortunately the ploy failed in this instance. Bad luck. It was also in evidence at Bristol City in 1999 / 2000 with almost a quarter of an hour extra time. Mind you, this was largely due to our midfielder, David Livermore, being in an "I could have been a contender" mode and decking all-comers with two confirmed KOs to his credit, including former Lion, Gerard Lavin. Well done. Bristol City didn't score here either so once again nice try ref, but tough cheddar.

Millwall's away following has its fair share of characters, as you can imagine. For example, there's one bloke who wears a cowboy style hat with all his away visit match tickets stuck in the hat band. There's also Dave, the bookie, who runs a gambling book on the coaches with bets about score predictions, etc,. He also wears a waistcoat to all the matches with hundreds of metal club badges on the front and "Up The Lions" emblazoned on the back in a Pearly King style.

But no one is more of a character than our own home and away companion, Mad Ted. Simon and I once had the privilege of being with him at Whitechapel station when he tried to start a row with 40 Leicester fans. Three versus 40, mmm, nice! He's sometimes called "Beth" due to the fact that he's from Bethnal Green. By the same process I'd be "Step" for Stepney and not because I'm a big fan of the Abba clones, honest. My usual companions, Pat and Simon, would be "Hack" for Hackney, Dave, Paul and Nathan would be "Ching" for Chingford and not because they've got a cough or are Chinese, and Clive would be "Romf" for Romford. I can't think what on Earth "Romf" could otherwise mean. Sorry. I've listed some of Ted's exploits throughout this book, however, I was thinking of writing a film screenplay of his life called *Mad Ted - Beyond The Kohlerdome*, with Mel Gibson as Ted. Inspired casting if I've ever seen it!

Apart from the typing error in the Gillingham programme (everyone knows Richard Sadlier's really 12 foot nine inches tall), the most bizarre programme notes I've ever read was at Cambridge in 1992. Cambridge United's manager at the time was John Beck. Now, apart from his predilection for administering cold showers to his players, he was instrumental in some of the most basic up and under agricultural hoofball it's ever been my pleasure (?) to see. Not so much "push and run" as "punt and go find it!"

In the kickabout prior to this game, for some reason Millwall's keeper, Aiden Davison, kept trying to knock the stewards over with well aimed kicks of the ball. The game itself consisted of trying to "moon launch" every ball, with most of them ending up in the surrounding countryside. This was played out to the backdrop of Millwall fans shouting "Higher, higher!" for every neck straining hoick.

Now bearing in mind the thinking that must go behind this type of tactic must be minimal at best, it left Mr Beck the brain capacity to write the only truly Zen inspired programme notes I've ever read. Try this for size: "You hold in your hand the camel's hair brush of a painter of life."

More Dalai Lama than Big Ron, I'm sure you'll agree. To add to the surrealness of it all, the PA blasted out "I've got a lovely bunch of coconuts!" at the end of the match. I know not why!

CHAPTER 4

THE MAN WITH THE PLASTIC BAGS

THE TITLE OF this chapter relates to a strange village idiot type man, shabbily dressed and clutching plastic Sainsbury's bags, who used to walk around the cinder track at Ipswich's Portman Road ground. Bizarrely, I witnessed this strange phenomenon on two separate occasions, and both times this weird looking creature would walk past the away fans penned in behind the goal and peer into the crowd as if he'd never encountered other humans before (some might say he still hadn't). He was greeted with chants of "Sex case, sex case, hang him, hang him, hang him!", a chant peculiar to Millwall as far as I know.

Now, I've come up with two theories as to what caused this strange behaviour. Perhaps it was because his family had only just released him from the attic a la *League Of Gentlemen*, or alternatively his puzzled expression was caused by the attire worn in the away section, which gave tantalising glimpses of a world of clothing outside of Oxfam shops.

Over the years, since football's become an entertainment and not a sport, a phenomenon has emerged - that of the club mascot. And a right old menagerie it is too. The sight of a grown man or woman (who knows?) poncing about inside a caricature of their club's image is a bit too Disneyland / Stuart Hall for me. I saw a veritable zoo of the creatures at Crystal Palace a few years ago, but what would you expect?

Now this may just be some weird hallucination on my part, but I'm sure I've recently seen two TV items about club muppets. Firstly I found out that there is a course that the creatures can go on to enhance their skills (!), run by some lovey who kept on referring to the sad buggers as "artistes". Pretentious, moi? Naturally the ideal location for such a course was The Valley, where else? And I saw an *It's A Knockout* style steeplejump featuring about 50 club creatures. I despair, I really do. Perhaps none of this is real and I should just lay off the booze.

Millwall have Zampa The Lion which isn't quite as bad as some. Derby's ram mascot? Watford's large hornet creature? The *It's A Knockout* style thing with a hat at Luton? Or H'Angus the monkey at

Hartlepool, whose first appearance was in our recent 1-0 FA Cup defeat. What's to stop Lord Lucan, Reggie Perrin or even Robert Maxwell (well perhaps not him - no club has a whale for a mascot does it?) hiding forever this way? Perhaps they already do?

The strangest incident in this drug induced pantomime was at Swansea for an FA Cup First Round 3-0 capitulation a couple of seasons ago. At this game the crowd was whipped into a lather anyway, and Cyril The Swan's urging and pitch invasion tactics led to him being charged with incitement. But what really summed up our pathetic showing perfectly was when in a half-time penalty shoot out between Zampa and Cyril, our mascot had to go off with an injury. It said it all for me, but that's me.

I think "real" half-time entertainment was provided a couple of years ago by Wolves' Wolfie fighting several Bristol City "creatures". Now if this caught on in a knockout competition to find the hardest club muppet, we'd have people paying for this spectacle alone. Just think – Zampa v Mr Potato Head Royle (What? That's his real head?) or against the West Ham Hammer Men. Now that is entertainment.

However, perhaps worse than the caricature muppets are the poor deluded souls who volunteer (?) to be undisguised mascots. At least behind a facade inside football's equivalent of a pantomime horse you are offered anonymity, but on my visits to Peterborough and Portsmouth, two foolhardy souls paraded their wares before the game. Quite what the purpose of their presence was, it's difficult to say. "Look, it's that prat again, let's get behind the team!" I think not. It does, however, give the away fans a target for their abuse, a bit like primal screaming for the masses.

At Peterborough, there is a "Posh" Man dressed in top hat and tails, "doffing his titfer" (I believe that's the expression). Quite how this came about, I can only guess. Did a drunken guest from an up-market wedding stray into the ground, and being a public schoolboy, thrived on the ridicule and stayed? Who knows.

The Portsmouth "Play up Pompey!" hello sailor type is obviously easier to understand due to its naval history, but I think they've taken "Kiss me Hardy" a bit too far in employing some limp wristed old queen dressed up in sailor's clobber who waves to the crowd and hoists his placard, "Ooh! missus." Why the supposition is that this display should result in anything but ridicule, I'm not sure.

Now, as the main bulk of a football crowd is still made up of working class men, at least in the real world of the Nationwide League, why the powers that be believe that letting young women parade around or perform at pre-game and half-time entertainment at matches will go by without sexual innuendo, I don't know. It might be a gentleman's club mentality in the Premiership (it could be - it's as expensive to join each of them), but it's still a building site "Hello darlin', give us a smile," sort of mentality at most other grounds.

For example, at Everton, girls wandered around the pitch dressed in old fashioned garb tossing toffees (Everton's nickname) into the crowd. As you would expect the response was "Get your tits out for the lads!", etc., much to the girls' obvious embarrassment. Seemed like a good idea, I suppose. I can also recall at Ipswich when the track side girls selling confectionery wore very short schoolgirl style skirts. Good idea given the mentality of your average fan, me included.

However one "performing girls" incident did bring a humorous moment. At Leicester a few years ago, Simon and I sat in the side seats whilst young American style pom-pom girls performed in mid pitch. Someone got up from our section and headed towards the front. Now presumably the steward assumed this man was on a perving mission because he hared down the stairs after him, only to trip over the pitch side barrier and fall flat on his face on the cinder track. A truly gratifying moment indeed, particularly for anyone who's had a run in with the "Little Hitlers".

I'm not sure the entertainment value of the next incident was meant or not, but for a night match at Wigan's Springfield Park for a heavily policed game, (riot police as is usual in our case), the home club had decided to get in extra stewards from what I can only assume to be the North West's only gay security service, because all the stewards were dressed in what could best be described as shocking pink coats. Lovely boys! It made me laugh anyway. "Hello, Butch Bouncers Limited. Can I help you?"

Not strictly entertainment, but an oddity anyway. How do the prat(s) at Portsmouth with the bell and trumpet get in the ground? And once in, how do they not get a lamping? One of life's great mysteries, I'd say. Also, at Chesterfield in 1999/2000 we were lambasted by another village idiot who looked like his entire wardrobe had come from a chain of Millets. Is this Derbyshire's idea of care in the community?

I know they say variety is dead (and praise the Lord, if some of the football related entertainment is anything to go on), and penalty shoot-outs, kids track racing and five-a-side matches are fine. At least they vaguely relate to football, but some misguided fool decided that a police dog handling display featuring black burglars being savaged by large rabid Alsations was suitable entertainment for our game at Tottenham a few years back. The crowd did enjoy it, but not for the wholesome reasons the organisers might have hoped.

In our second season in the top Division, at a time when we were going down quicker than Brian Rix's trousers, we played at Aston Villa and lost 1-0 in a pretty uneventful game. However, one of our then very recent ex-players, Tony Cascarino, was playing one of his first games for the Villa. He'd done the old "leaving the sinking ship" routine and consequently was less than popular when he appeared on the pitch in claret and blue - another red rag to a bull for us due to the Hammers' colours connection.

I'm sure he must have loved every second of his 90 minute "Judas!" barracking. You could visibly see his heart sinking every time he had to come near us. Bad luck. He shouldn't have left us should he? "Loyalty? No, sorry, don't know that one."

I've only been to Huddersfield once, in April, 1996, to their brand spanking new stadium. I missed our 4-0 Cup thrashing of them as I was in America at the time. When I saw us play there we were still in the new Division One, but well into our "shoot yourself in the foot" mood. At this time only three stands had been built, with the opposite end to us being a big hole giving panoramic views of t'Yorkshire. This is the only stadium of this kind I'd seen up close, a stadium design to my mind more akin to a bridge than a football ground, but that's just my opinion. It seems like a waste of seats to have curved roofs, but it's an award winning structure so what do Prince Charles and I know? Still the Lloyds Building in the City of London is also an architectural wonder of the age and that looks like a petro-chemical plant to me, so there.

My first trip to Nottingham Forest for a 3-1 defeat in the old Division One holds the record for the longest time to get a programme. In fact in an act full of determination, we had to be let into the home stand with a pack of bloodhounds in tow in an effort to track the illusive buggers down. Nothing important, just thought I'd mention it.

My first visit to Hillsborough, a 3-0 defeat in our first season in the old Division One which I've detailed elsewhere, was also notable for our return trip, when one of our fellow passengers gave us all a running comedy skit on Millwall being the "young pretenders to the Championship throne." He carried this on practically all the way back to London, in a cross between Stuart Hall and Alan Whicker, if you can imagine such a thing. I've not done it justice here, but it had us all in fits all the way home.

28

At Charlton a few years ago, when Lee Bowyer still played for them, the team pen pictures inside the programme filled my head with thoughts of banjo music, due to the gorgeous pairing of Robinson and Bowyer bearing an uncanny resemblance to the duelling banjo pluckers in *Deliverance*. I wouldn't stand by a tree if you see these two with a length of rope if I were you. If you've seen the film, I think you'll understand my drift.

For some reason I've twice had the dubious pleasure of seeing the band of the Grenadier Guards - once at Wrexham a couple of seasons ago, when on a day that resembled a monsoon, the band came into the stand next to us and played Cockney knees-up type favourites to raise our soggy spirits in a dire 0-0 game. Gives a new meaning to the phrase "a seat near the band".

Much more alarmingly, I saw them prior to this at Wolverhampton for a night match in 1993. At this match Wolves were celebrating the opening of the Billy Wright Stand. I was treated (?) to the sights and sounds of The Beverley Sisters accompanied by the Guards band performing *I Love To Go A-Wandering*. Well so do I, and I headed straight for the sanctuary of the toilet on the assumption that it would be quieter in there. Unfortunately, in an act of sadism not bettered outside of a Japanese POW camp, the bastards had installed a PA in the loos, so not only did I hear the show, but in full stereophonic glory.

For some spooky reason, all my trips to Wolves have coincided with either stand closures, topping-outs, or grand openings of stands. Weird, eh?

Fortunately, given the torture that was The Beverley Sisters, I've not seen many "celebrity" days at football. I've seen "operatic beanpole", Russell Watson, give us the Pavarotti treatment at Preston in 1999/2000, I've seen the Michael Bentt charade at The Den, and Billy Schwer "Who the fucking hell are you?"d at Luton, and I do remember as a child seeing Alf Garnet at West Ham in full Hammers garb v Tottenham. But by far the strangest was an open topped presidential style drive around St Andrews by soap superstar, Amy Turtle (*Crossroads*' charlady for the younger amongst you). This really whipped the Brummies into a frenzy prior to our 1972 table topper, I can tell you.

However, the most ill advised visit was by Barbara Windsor at Derby to draw a half-time lottery in the old First Division, in a game that effectively relegated us to Division One / Two. It's so confusing, isn't it? She was in the throws of a split with her criminal husband, Ronnie Knight, who'd disappeared to somewhere in Spain. I'm sure her recuperation was greatly helped by our chants of "Where's your Ronnie gone?", *Una Paloma Blanca*, and *Y Viva Espana*. You get the idea. Still, if we can help somebody along the way and all that.

CHAPTER 5

MUSHY PEAS AND CURRY SAUCE

MY ABIDING EARLY memory of going to football is usually accompanied with the smell and sound of the hot dog and hamburger stalls that used to line your route on the way to the ground, an aroma and sight that will probably live with me forever. Should you take your life in your hands in the food equivalent of Russian Roulette? Should you actually buy something? The stalls were naturally spotlessly clean, had certificates of public hygiene and were salmonella free, obviously.

The most adventurous choice was a hot dog, because it was immersed in a none too appertising yellow coloured liquid and offered the most risk for any of the thrill seekers out there. I saw an awesome sight when I was a child on one of my regular family holidays to Great Yarmouth when I came across the king of hot dogs, the Westler 12 incher, or Donkey Dick Special as you could call it. Now that is a hot dog!

Not "away", but food related, The Old Den had the fastest peanut seller in all Christendom. In the 60s it was usual to buy bags of Percy Dalton peanuts still in their shells, usually sold outside and inside the ground. This gave you something to do during the more tedious parts of the match, when you could shell your nuts and add to the peanut shell strewn floor that on a good day could be knee deep. At The Den the seller was like a cross between the Artful Dodger and Speedy Gonzalez as he'd weave his way through the crowd with his cry of "Peanuts! Peanuts!!"

By the time you tracked him down he'd usually gone. At it's worst it was usually necessary to lay an elaborate set of traps in an effort to slow him down and to actually buy something. All seater stadiums seem to have been the death knell of the peanut seller. God bless 'em.

Unfortunately, in my many years of away travelling, it's been necessary to sample the local culinary delights and as you can imagine, Egon Ronay territory it isn't. That said, for some reason the pies "up north" seem to be better than ours "dahn sarf", with more variety too. I've not sampled the delights at The Den, however, as I prefer to poison myself with my own cooking.

That aside, I did encounter a little too much variety for even my Catholic tastes on a trip to Everton. Simon and I travelled up on a club coach for a midweek League Cup second leg game in 1995 which we won 4-2. Big Five, pah! It's a long journey, we were running late and we arrived at the ground unfed a couple of minutes before kick-off. As soon as we got in the ground, we headed straight for the refreshment counter and ordered a pie each.

"What pies are they mate?" we asked.

"Meat", came the reply.

"Yes, but what meat?" we continued.

"Er, meat" came the response.

Oh, that's alright then. As they say, beggars can't be choosers and as kick-off was imminent, we took the pies and headed to our seats. All was fine until the first bite. We were greeted with a spray of hot pork fat. A hot pork pie? This may well be a northern delicacy, I couldn't say, but it was a bit much for our Southern softie palates. We had a struggle, but as were starving we managed somehow to finish them amidst much trepidation. For some reason I've yet to see this delicacy appear on *Masterchef*. Strange that. And here's a tip if you arrive in London at about 3.00 to 3.30am. Don't wear a Millwall shirt as we did after the Everton game, as taxis won't pick you up funnily enough.

In 1972, I travelled to Birmingham. I've detailed this trip later on, so I'll not go on about it, but I lost my friends at Euston and they went up without me. They told me of an incident later on when I saw them. They got off the train and headed for the nearest café. The walls were running with condensation, the windows were steamed up and vapour rose thickly from the pie cabinet. A Brummie then approached the counter and said "Are them pies hot?", much to the bemused looks of the counter staff.

I went to Blackburn in the 1990s. All was fine until I visited the food stall and ordered my customary pie. I was actually thinking of writing the definitive book, *Pies Of The Nationwide League*. Perhaps later. Anyway the girl behind the counter gave me my pie and I gave her a note. For some reason at Blackburn they had a tomato ketchup tray. Usefully, the girl in an attempt to give me my change, managed to drop it in the ketchup, prompting me to ferret about for several minutes in the sticky mess to retrieve it. Very hygienic, I'm sure. It also left me looking like an abattoir worker on National Cowslaughtering Day.

Some refreshment stalls give off a message, and that subliminal message is "Don't say I didn't warn you." One such was at

Ayresome Park, Middlesbrough. Again, after a long journey I headed straight for the grub. I waded through the burger and pie strewn floor that surrounded the stall. I got my order and was very soon adding to the floor decoration myself. The food was crap, quite literally possibly! But I'm sure you could get an Arts Council grant, if not a Turner Prize, for "The Food Mountains Of The Western World" montage, which the general area around the refreshment stand beautifully displayed.

At Luton, most of us left a restaurant without paying. Serves them right for rioting. Oh no, that was us wasn't it? Sorry, my mistake.

We went to Bolton in the 1993 season, came out of the station and hunted for a chip shop. We found one and discovered the real difference between Londoners and Northerners. In London, if you buy something and chips you invariably get it wrapped up in paper with salt and vinegar, or for the more adventurous, ketchup, that's all. "Up north", we had a cardboard tray, wooden fork, mushy peas and curry sauce, with ketchup, brown sauce, mustard and God alone knows what else as optional extras. Who said there's not a great cultural culinary divide?

After a 5-1 midweek League Cup defeat at West Bromwich in 1983, we left the ground, got in our car, and after a tour of Wolverhampton - by mistake I can assure you - we headed towards London via a stop off for comfort food at Watford Gap services. We arrived at the same time as the club coaches. It was obviously National Food Tasting Day because everyone picked up food from the counter, took a bite and put it back. Still, it serves them right for trying to stitch you up like a kipper at every opportunity. I don't know why somebody doesn't come clean and open a Dick Turpin Highway Robbery chain of service station restaurants. A bit of candour would go a long way. Maybe "come and taste Dick's whopper" is a bit too candid!

We went to Macclesfield for a midweek game. We only had about 200 fans there, most for curiosity value and what a curiosity it was. As I mentioned previously, irrespective of our low turn out, the refreshment stall continued to cook all night. The usual burger, sausage, chips, hot dog type stylee, but enough to feed a small army. Maybe someone had added a nought to our expected figure, so they cooked in preparation for a fleet of late arriving Londoners. Could be, or perhaps they were moonlighting as outside caterers, who knows.

Simon and I travelled to Derby for a match in the 90s. As we went by train and we didn't have to get a particular train back, we went wandering around to find some food. We found a Chinese restaurant called something like The Cherry Orchard. Very Checkov! Being the adventurous types, we ordered chicken and chips to go. Simon picked up a take away menu and took it home to his wife in Hackney. When he got home, he told her of a new Chinese he'd found. She said she would call and get some food which she did, much to the bewilderment of the people in Derby about to set out on a 150 mile chicken chow mein mercy dash.

I've eaten a pasty in Plymouth that was about the size of a large loaf and witnessed a pie shop in the ground at York, but by far the strangest thing we've encountered was at Rotherham in the 90s. Simon and I travelled up on the club coach. We arrived at Rotherham, a town that, around the ground at least, looked like a rusty scrap heap. We'd arrived very early before the turnstiles had opened, so we had a wander around, but couldn't find any food places we liked the look of, so we went back to the stadium and were eventually let into the ground.

We headed straight for the refreshments stall as soon as it opened. We ordered our coffees, etc and we got chatting to the middle aged women working behind the counter. Nothing unusual there you might think, and obviously you'd be right, but bearing in mind that this woman didn't know us from Adam and we'd not been formally introduced, the topic of conversation was a tad racy to say the least. After the initial pleasantries, she proceeded to give us a sexual history of her whole family, particularly her parents. She went into obscene and graphic detail about the quality and quantity of her parents' bedroom antics, cataloguing the contents of her knickers drawer, and giving us a "blow by blow" account, if you'll pardon the expression, of all the sex aids that she'd bought her parents over the years, discussing their personal preferences and more. A bit much on an empty stomach, I can tell you.

"Well Mabel, is it the Pifco Mega Deluxe Twin Speed 12 incher or the Big Boy multi throbber tonight?"

Thank God she didn't have any photos on her of the antics. I think she took the "Northerners are more friendly" theory a bit far! It certainly opened, and watered, our eyes to the delights of the geriatric swinger scene in Yorkshire, I can tell you. This was undoubtedly the highlight of a dreadful game, which ended 0-0 and contained the worst close-in miss, by a Rotherham player, I've ever seen.

CHAPTER 6

KARAOKE DAYS AND NIGHTS

As an insight into a club's mentality, I believe the chants it invents, or uses, give a pretty good idea of the fans' mind set. Quite what Freud, or you, will make of the following I've no idea. As a background to these chants, it is important to realise certain things are held to be true at The Den:

1) All blonde players are obviously gay and are fair game.
2) All people even remotely outside London are either bumpkins, sheepshaggers or northern bastards.
3) All northerners wear flat caps, live on cobbled streets like the old Coronation Street, breed and race pigeons, have a whippet and walk to work, usually up a steep incline, to the strains of a Hovis brass band style accompaniment.
4) All stewards have either "eaten all the pies", should show us "her tits" or are child molesters.
5) All people of non-London origin should be abused irrespective of geographical accuracy of abuse.
6) Any opposing players' or managers' foibles, no matter how tragic or personal, are "open season".

I've tried to give you a taste of what it is to be Millwall. I've tried to add a note showing origin home or away, alternative uses and accompanying sign language if appropriate. Think of it as a sort of abuser's master class.

West Ham at Upton Park a couple of weeks after Bobby Moore's death, this was sung at a game Millwall led 1-0, only for West Ham to score two goals in a matter of minutes after its first performance. What inspired them, I don't know.

**"Bobby Moore, Bobby Moore, riding through the glen,
Bobby Moore, Bobby Moore, he had sex with men,
Queer as a cunt,
Take's it up the bum,
Bobby Moore, Bobby Moore, is no more."**
(sung to Robin Hood theme)

West Ham's response was to say "No one liked us" because we were scum. A bit harsh, what?

Also at West Ham, the aptly named club photographer, Mr Bacon, was greeted with "Have you ever seen your cock?", due to his immense bulk.

Liverpool (Anfield) at our first visit in the old Division One, a few notable chants here:

"Who the fucking hell are you?"
Not original, I know, but quite ironic nonetheless, as Liverpool were the country's top side at the time.

"Does the social know you're here?"
"Loads and loadsa money!"
"You'll never get a job!"
All general social deprivation songs to imply London's superiority (applies to all northern clubs).

"I'd rather be a Paki than a Scouse!"
Make up your own meaning.

Chelsea (performed at Brentford) days after Chelsea's director had died in a helicopter crash:

"Blue is the colour,
Football is the game,
Poor old Matthew Harding
Should have caught a train!"

Bristol City (at Bristol) 1999/2000:

"I can't read, I can't write, but I can drive a tractor,
I'm a Bristol City fan and I'm a fucking wanker!"

This is obviously sung to show our urban sophistication. It was sung at Ashton Gate for about half an hour non-stop, to a "Cotton Eyed Joe" type rhythm, much to bemused looks from the locals (note - also sung at Bristol Rovers).

Luton Town (at Luton): As Luton's ground is in a predominantly Asian area, this is the usual type of abuse:

"You live in a corner shop!"
"You'll run back to Bangladesh!"
"Stand up if you hate curry!"
I abstained from the last chant. I may be abusive, but I'm not a hypocrite!

Gillingham (at Gillingham) last season and always. I don't know Kent personally, but usual assertions would imply it is populated by caravan dwellers.

"You live in a caravan!"
"Where's your caravan?"
In the past also sung at Terry Hurlock pre-Millwall days.

"Two nil and you fucked it up!"
After defeat by Man City in play-offs, 1999.

"You've only got one leg!" to a player on a stretcher, who'd just collided with a post at our end and the sympathetic, "Let the fucking Gypo die!"

In response we were greeted with "You live in a tower block / council flat!" and "Two nil and you fucked it up!" after we let a two goal lead slip against The Gills at The Den in 2000.

Middlesbrough (Ayresome Park) during the height of the Cleveland child abuse scandal:

"Sex case, sex case, hang him, hang him, hang him!"
"You sleep with your sister's kids!"
Please note, can also be used to abuse suspect looking stewards.

Western / Welsh teams (general):

"Sheep, sheep, sheep shaggers!"
"Ooh Arr! You're all sheep shaggers!"
"Ooh Arr! Ambrosia!"
If required, you can add bleating style sheep noises.

37

Brighton & Hove Albion, home and away in the Worthington Cup this season, and we were excelling ourselves in the homophobic department with numerous gay references. Save for Tom Robinson and the line in *The Flintstones* about having "a gay old time", we had the lot.

"Sing when you're mincing! You only sing when you're mincing!"
"Does your mother know you're queer?"
"Does your boyfriend know you're here?"
"I'd rather be a paki than a poof!"
"Faggots, faggots, what's the score?"
"You're queer and you know you are!"
"Do you take it up the arse?"
"You're queer and your wife's a man!"
"Up the rear, up the rear, up the rear!"
"Stand up if your arse is sore!"
"Suck his knob, suck his knob, suck his knob!"
(to physio tending to injured Brighton player at The Den)
"Denzil, Denzil, watch your arse!"
"Mum knows you swallow, does your Mum know you swallow?"
And finally, **"Vaseline, Vaseline, Vaseline!"**

Quite a selection, I'm sure you'll agree. Unfortunately, for the home leg I was sitting next to Simon's daughter, Lisa, who is 11, and she asked me what some of the chants meant. Blustering, I managed to pass that one back to Simon quick sharp, I can tell you.

Ipswich Town in the Worthington Cup 2000 away. Due to home town Premiership refereeing, Millwall only had seven men on the pitch at one point so . . .
"Denzil, Denzil, on his own, Denzil on his own . . . "
"Five-a-side, five-a-side, five-a-side!"
"Are you happy, referee? Are you happy, referee?" (not an enquiry about his well being either, I can assure you!)

Grimsby (Old Den) in a night match when they thrashed us 6-1:

"You only sing when you're fishing!"
Note can also be used for "yokel" teams, substituting the word "farming" for "fishing".

38

Crystal Palace (home or away):

"Ooh! Ah! Eric Cantona!"
after his "appalling" attack on that nice Palace fan.
"Palace, Palace, who the fuck are Palace?"
for a Selhurst Park win, at the time of the Roy Chubby Brown and
Smokey classic.

Kenny Dalglish (Old Den) when Liverpool manager had a habit of
standing up the whole game:

"Dalglish can't sit down, he's got piles!"
I don't know about piles, he's certainly got bundles!

Paul Gascoigne (Tottenham) at White Hart Lane, sung by 7,000
away fans, to which the loveable scamp put the ball up his shirt and
lay down, pregnant woman style, on the pitch: "You fat cunt!"

Paul Peschisolido (Fulham) or anyone he plays for, husband of
Karen Brady, who's not liked at Millwall after St Andrews game
trouble: "You're shit and you're wife's a slag!" News to him I think,
usually accompanied by references to his wife's sexual proclivities.

Peter Shilton (Southampton) after a sex slur and wife beating
allegations: "Shilton beats his wife up!"

Ian Wright (Arsenal) at New Den, when before an FA Cup game he
said on Arsenal's Club Call that all Millwall fans were racist. This
was also published in the morning papers. Now call me cynical, but
you can explain this outburst in several ways:
1) He's right (no pun intended)
2) His timing is idiotic to say the least
3) His purposes was to turn home crowd away from supporting
Millwall in order to abuse him.
As the following was practically all that was sung all afternoon, you
decide: "Ian wank, wank, wank, Ian wank, wank, wank . . . "

Barry Fry (Birmingham) New Den after ill advised goal celebrations
at trouble strewn St Andrew's game:

"Die, die, Barry Fry!"
Given added weight by the fact that he's got a dicky ticker.

Northern teams (home or away) "The Hovis theme", an old favourite, this one
"Go to the pub, drink ten pints, get absolutely plastered,
Go back home, beat up the wife, 'cause I'm a northern bastard!"
Unlike Mr Wright, sweeping stereotyping is not our game, oh no.

Referees (general). It's always good to have a few anti-ref chants, as general incompetence on their part tends to exhaust them quite quickly:
"Referee, Referee, your old lady is a whore, your old lady is a whore!"
An old stalwart of the 60s and 70s this one
"Cheat, Cheat, Cheat!"
to highlight perceived conspiracy theory against us. It's true I tell you, they're on orders not to let us win you know!
"The referee's a wanker!"
"Who's the wanker in the black?"
Self explanatory, and abusing, these two.

Mark McGhee (Wolves) 1990s. A man who is now Millwall's manager, but who at the time had gone rapidly through more clubs than George Best and Tiger Woods put together. Your choice:

"Mark McGhee's blue, yellow, red, green, black and white army!"

Unknown black player (Notts County) and to subsequent "lippy" black players (note "lippy", as most racist abuse tends to be tied to some perceived misdemeanour on a player's part and not just random because we are all racists)
"Day-o, day-o, daylight come and me want go home!"
Not a bastion of political correctness, The Den I'm afraid.

Jim Leighton (Manchester United) at Old Trafford. Not a chant, but a couple of astute observations made to Man U's then undead and bowlegged keeper: "Oi, haggis bollocks! Did they model the Channel Tunnel on your legs?"

The police (not the band), always welcome home or away:

"Kill, kill, kill the Bill!"

**"Harry Roberts is our friend, is our friend, is our friend,
Harry Roberts is our friend, he kills coppers,
Let him out to kill some more, kill some more, kill some more,
Let him out to kill some more, Harry Roberts!"**

Laurel And Hardy theme as they walk past, always an old stalwart.

"We hate Old Bill and we hate Old Bill!"
Another old favourite.

Millwall, any time, any place, anywhere. Just a flavour of the rich verbal culture that exists. First a comment, not a chant, between two Millwall arguing behind me at Old Den:
"You can shut up or I'll have ya. You're just about my handwriting!"
Glad he's not my handwriting, or he'd be a very mixed-up, indecipherable sort of chap.

"Let him die, let him die, let him die!"
to opposition players giving it the dying swan "I'm in agony" routine. Also the anthem of the National Association Of Funeral Directors, I believe!

"We are evil!"
An old stalwart, sung to the tune of the *Volga* boat song, more like vulgar though in our case.

"You'll never make the station!"
Or find it, in some cases.

"You're going home in a fucking ambulance!"
I'm assuming a fucking ambulance isn't a nurse staffed mobile brothel, but I don't know. Otherwise self explanatory I think.

"Now you're going to believe us, we couldn't give a fuck!"
"On the piss, on the piss, on the piss!"
Sung at Den during 4-1 defeat, the day we received Division Two Championship.

**"The (insert your team here) sing, we don't know why,
Because after the game they're going to die!"**
Lovely sentiments, I'm sure you'll agree.

"You'll run, and you know you will!"
Ditto.

"Oh! East London is like Bengal, it's like the back streets of Delhi!"
Not around my house, it's not!

"You couldn't score in a brothel!"
To incompetent forwards who on some days couldn't score even if the brothel in question was in the final of the Miss Whiplash Cup.

"The Lions, The Lions, da da da da da da da da da da war / roar!"
Who knows?

"We laugh at the (your name here)!"
Sung at away fans and first heard when Birmingham didn't show up for a return bout after the St Andrew's trouble.

Strange one the following, which doesn't bear visualising.   An old 60s/70s favourite:
"We'll be running round (town name) with our willies hanging out, we'll be running around   (town name) with our willies hanging out! Singing I've got a bigger one than you, no you ain't!"
I wouldn't have thought it wise to run around anywhere up north during winter with anything hanging out for obvious reasons.

"We're the best behaved supporters in the land,
We're the best behaved supporters in the land,
We're the best behaved supporters, best behaved supporters,
We're the best behaved supporters in the land - when we win!
We're a right bunch of bastards when we lose . . . !"
I told you irony wasn't lost on us!

"Bye bye (your name here), bye bye (your name here)!"
"Fuck off (your name here), fuck off (your name here)!"
Please accompany with Queen Mother style hand waving.

"Cartman's gonna get you!"
to Bury keeper, "Kenny", in 2000 season.

"Denzil's got a big one!"
Millwall's keeper, Tony Warner is a Scouser, and bears a marked resemblance to Denzil in *Only Fools And Horses* and *The Full Monty* bloke called Horse, so an apt chant in all ways as good old Tone's supposed to have a big willy. Good for him.
"Who you gonna call? Nosebusters."
Sung at The Old Den to tune of *Ghostbusters*, how jolly violent.

"Fuck 'em all, fuck 'em all,
United, West Ham, Liverpool,
'Cos we are the Millwall and we are the best.
We are the Millwall so fuck all the rest!"
Not solely a Millwall chant, but together with the "No one likes us!" chant, sums up Millwall's mentality perfectly.

"You live in a pigeon loft!"
"Home to your ferrets, you're going home to your ferrets!"
Sung at Notts County. Well it's up north to us, hence the stereotyped northern hobby references. For variety can use "whippet" if required for "ferret".

"Give me an M, give me an I . . . " to spell out Millwall, an old chestnut this one. For some bizarre reason we always say "Wubble U" for "W", I know not why. Given a classic rendition once at The Old Den, when the leader of the chant forgot how to spell Millwall in mid chant and ground to a halt to much derisory laughter, as you can imagine.

The New Den's C.B.L. (South Stand) choirmaster in recent seasons is an old stager everyone calls Grandad. He's usually implored to give us a song. I wish one day he'd break into *My Way* or *I Left My Heart In San Francisco*. That would be funny. He also has the following chants directed at him:
"Grandad is our leader!"
"Grandad's on viagra!"

For reference, it's a great Millwall tradition to sing all the way through any announcements made over the tannoy at away grounds. Usually with the drone chant "Miiiilllllwaaall!", irrespective of the announcement - ie. "The ground's on fire!", "We're at war, the four minute warning's gone off!". Doesn't matter a jot to us, oh no!

43

"You don't come from round 'ere, you don't come from round 'ere, ooh arr! Ooh arr!"
Sung to Norwich City at The New Den in a recent friendly, performed to our country cousins in a mock *Archers* / Bernard Matthews accent. Bootiful!

Naturally over the years all our abuse hasn't been without it's riposte, but before I mention some of these, a few queries . . .
Why do Stoke sing *Delilah*?
What's Chelsea got to do with men mowing?
How do Northampton seriously sing "Come on you cobblers"?
What's a gashead?
But stranger than any of the above, a chant heard at Watford about Luton manager, David Pleat. At our match at Vicarage Road we were serenaded with "David Pleat's a wanker, he wears a wanker's hat . . . "
Quite how it went after that I don't know as I was trying to imagine this particular item of head wear. Now I'm obviously not aware of all makes and types of head gear you can buy, but I've never personally seen a "wanker's hat", particularly not at Dunn & Co. I did consider a couple of possibilities:
1) Perhaps it comes equipped with a dirty mag, man sized tissues and rubber gloves, or . . .
2) Perhaps it has a reinforced back piece to prevent damage from any over excited headboard related injuries.
Your guess is as good as mine, but I do feel the nation must be told.
Like the anti songs we sing, the usual thing for opposing fans is to pick on a stereotype, so . . .

"Leave it out, leave it out!"
"Awright, awright, awright!"
"Rent boys, rent boys, la de da de dah!"
"The water in Majorca!"
"Millwall Millwall southern scum! Millwall southern scum!"
"Hello, hello! Cockney rent boys, Cockney rent boys, hello . . . "
And the perennial, **"We hate Cockneys!"**

The first four chants were directed at us in Derby and Leicester, the next two at Preston. The Cockney chants apply as soon as we leave The Smoke, irrespective of direction.

"There's only one Arthur Scargill!"
At Derby in response to our politically observed chant, "Where have all your miners gone?"

At Cardiff, Swansea and Wrexham, we were greeted with "Argentina! Argentina!", a reference to England's World Cup defeat. Have I missed something? Didn't the Welsh Guards fight in the Falklands?

And again at Cardiff, this post devolution gem . . .
"You can stick the fucking Queen up your arse!"
A career in showbiz awaits if you could, I think.

At Man City a couple of seasons ago . . .
"One nil, two nil, three nil, in your Cup Final!"
It was actually only one score at a time, but changed each time we capitulated. This obviously implies that Man City are the big fish who we were privileged to play. It was pointed out that if they were any good, they wouldn't actually be in Division Three!

"Town full of Munichs, it's just a town full of Munichs!"
Maybe so, but we're not glory hunting Man Utd fans, so what's it got to do with us?

In the 90s Division One days we had the following chant sung at us by all and sundry:
"Millwall are going nowhere!"
That's where you're wrong, we're going into free-fall and financial administration, so there.

I hope this chapter shows that the English's talent for great song writing is still alive and well.

CHAPTER 7

£1 A PINT, HOW MUCH?

WHEN WE'VE DRIVEN to away trips, we've sometimes visited pubs near to the ground. I wouldn't recommend this at certain grounds, Millwall being one of them, but if you're careful it's usually okay. I have heard some horror stories about being trapped in pubs when heavily outnumbered and then attacked, or of being lured back to the pub after the game by seemingly friendly locals, only for it to turn nasty later on. I've listed a few of the more memorable visits for your consumption.

The title of this chapter refers to a visit to Walsall's old ground in September, 1984, where we drew 3-3 in a Division Three game. Steve Kimberley and I drove to this game. He was an old school mate who I used to go to games with at the time. Around this period we drove to quite a few away matches and for this particular match we arrived at about 1.00pm.

We decided to head for the nearest boozer - not me, but the pub. We ordered a couple of pints and were charged £1.20 for them. We looked at each other, and being honest sorts of chaps we said to the barman, "You've only charged us for one pint, mate."

"No that's right, it's 60p a pint."

We looked shocked and he said, "Why, where do you two come from?"

We said, "London, it's a pound a pint there."

The barman was stunned. He called all the locals over and made us repeat this amazing revelation. The locals were left mumbling about their luck in not living in "The Smoke".

Steve and I also drove to York on a freezing day to see a 1-1 draw in the same season. Lovely place, very historic and chock full of pubs. We again got there quite early and were ushered into a pub with the words, "Quick, get inside before the Millwall arrive."

We decided not to inform them that they already had.

The same thing happened several years later at Southend in a pub on the seafront, when even though a few of us were wearing colours, we were still told to "Get in before Millwall get here, we're going to lock the doors."

You can imagine our distress. "A lock-in, oh my God". Still although this dampened our spirits, no pun intended, we somehow managed to get through the ordeal.

The usual response to a Millwall visit is to put bouncers on the door, board up the windows, lock up your daughters and head for the hills, hence the above reaction. Usually if you did get in at all, once they twigged your accent the mood changed. We didn't even get past the doors in Cambridge or Oxford at this time.

For the vital relegation match at Chesterfield, which I've highlighted in other chapters, we had a drink in a pub near to the ground. This was full of Millwall.

The publican asked, "How many of you lot are coming up today?" "About 4,000".

"Bollocks you are!" he said in disbelief.

It was precisely at this moment in a "timing" event that only usually happens in TV sitcoms that we opened the pub door just as the trains arrived, and we witnessed a blue and white mass moving "wildebeest" like towards the ground. This wiped the look off his face, I can tell you. We won 1-0 in front of 4,000 Millwall and about 200 locals. As Bob Hoskins might have said, "It's good to be a smug bastard."

We've been in many pubs over the years where Millwall have taken the place over without a local in sight. This has obviously been fine with us, but sometimes we've been fortunate in the choice of pub we've picked. Some examples . . .

On a trip to Bolton in 1993 we thought that as we were quite early, we would get some food and find a pub. We had a wander about, rejected one pub in the High Street and found a back street pub. It was a "local" type of old fashioned pub. When we stood at the bar we were "earholed" by a club colours bedecked village idiot type who, for some reason, supported Bolton even though he came from Twyford. This was the only threat in the bar. However, when we left the pub and headed to the ground, we walked past the previously rejected pub, luckily as it turned out, because we found that this pub was Meathead Central, full of locals busily scouting the streets for passing Millwall.

In 1983, Millwall played First Division West Bromwich Albion at home in a first leg League Cup game and won 3-0. We went up to The Hawthorns for the midweek second leg clash, sure of victory. Consequently 5,000 travelled up that night. Steve K and I again drove up and we again arrived early, so we went into the nearest pub to the ground. We were standing in a mostly empty bar when a mob of locals arrived outside making dire threats and also making a valiant attempt to storm the pub. Unbeknownst to us, the publican was in the habit of locking the doors to home fans and only letting away fans in. Good man! This event eventually passed off peacefully and in fact, closer to kick-off, the pub was full of Millwall.

This was a game notable for the home team getting pelted with bananas due to their large black playing contingent, a punch up on the lower roof of a side stand, and for West Brom kicking their way, referee assisted, to a 5-1 win.

The roughest pub I've ever been in away was at Wolverhampton. Not far from the station is a Banks pub which had the following selling points:

1) No carpet
2) No furniture to speak of
3) Boarded up windows
4) Bouncers on the door
5) A police van parked outside

Thankfully the beer was okay. This is the place to take your girlfriend for a romantic night out, no doubt. Not a hint of trouble here.

I've spoken to a West Ham fan I know who had visited the same pub more recently. He said it was still exactly the same. Still, it's probably a "sight" of historical importance or outstanding natural beauty or something and can't be touched.

Away from football, but still pub related, the most frightening sight I've seen was in Edinburgh. An old mate of mine, Paul, drove us both up to Scotland to see England play in the Rugby Union World Cup Semi-Final at Murrayfield. We parked the car a couple of streets away from the ground and went to a nearby pub. When we first got there it was early and the pub was half empty. Nobody said anything about our non-Scottish accents, but as the time wore on and more Scots arrived, it was becoming pretty obvious that we were less than welcome - although Paul's actually Welsh.

Before we left, I decided to go to the toilet and went to the urinal. In there, the true horror struck me. I was the only one in trousers, and the sight of a load of hairy arsed Scotsman lifting their kilts to relieve themselves was enough to chill even the most sturdy Englishmen's blood. Pale faced, we left the pub and went to the ground. What we found was a "dry" Murrayfield, where the entertainment consisted of two hours of "cat strangling", or massed pipe bands as they're called.

If you're a Londoner in London and not wearing club colours, it's usually okay as you obviously speak the same as the locals and therefore blend in. However, it was in London that I've encountered the only up-close threat of violence.

After home games at Cold Blow Lane, we used to drink in the home pubs or go up to the Old Kent Road. Sometimes we'd come east to my domain. Two other mates, Micky and his brother Steve, come from the East End as well, so we knew the pubs.

We went to Upton Park to see Millwall play Charlton when they were in their wanderlust phase. Five of us came back on the tube to Mile End station and went to one of our usual haunts on the other side of the main road. We had a couple of pints and decided to go for a bit of a crawl. We crossed the road to a pub called The Horn Of Plenty (now a Firkin pub). This is almost next door to the station and it's perceived to be a West Ham pub, which Millwall have attacked in the past, but we were playing Charlton so it didn't occur to us to expect anything.

However, as soon as we walked into the pub, this giant of a bloke crashed into Micky. Now, Micky is six foot two, and at that time was about 20 stone. This bloke barged him a couple of times saying "Come on West Ham, let's have it!" As we weren't sure who this bloke or the other dozen "tooled up" men emerging from the back room were, Micky simply said he wasn't West Ham and didn't elaborate. Luckily before the carnage started, one of their number recognised some of us as Millwall and called off the attack. They then proceeded to ask us if we fancied joining them in their Hammers hunt. We declined, saying "No thanks, we're only out for a beer."

After a short time they all left, we stayed in the pub playing pool and drinking before our next stop. The barmaid in the pub was amazed to see us unbattered. She said that the Millwall had been blocking off the exits and stockpiling weapons in the back room, so ironically the only real danger I've ever, nearly, been in was at a "local" and from my own fans. One postscript to this event - a bloke we knew came into the bar a few minutes after our would-be assailants' departure. Luckily for him he missed all the fun, particularly as he was wearing a Tottenham shirt. What his fate might have been, God knows. This was a very, very lucky escape for all of us - surprised, unarmed and outnumbered. Not my favourite position to be in.

CHAPTER 8

GONE WEST –
SEAGULL BOMBING RUNS

SOME AWAY TRIPS take on the appearance of a highly implausible comedy script. One such trip was to Plymouth in 1996. This trip bore more than a passing resemblance to John Cleese's *Clockwise*.

I've been to Plymouth three times, usually on the club's trains via the Dawlish coast and very picturesque it is too! For all of these visits, I've stood on a largeish open terrace at Home Park, have never seen Millwall win, and have suffered from the highly accurate seagull bombing missions carried out above our heads. Peculiarly this only seems to happen at the away end. Perhaps they bait the terrace with fish prior to our arrival, or more sinisterly, the seagulls are radio controlled. Is this possible, do you think? These events aren't my imagination, honest. It's actually on one of Millwall's end of season videos.

For this particular visit, I'd arranged to go to the game with an old school friend, Colin Briden. Colin comes from the same part of the East End as me. He first started to go to Millwall as a child with his dad, and as we both went to the same secondary school with a large contingent of boys from Rotherhithe, Bermondsey and Dog Island, we used to go mob handed to games together when old enough. I was best man at his wedding and am godparent to his son, Chris. He now lives in Bridport in Dorset. I have to give him a detailed account of all the matches and he's also got the internet to check the accuracy of my rambling 'phone reports. Anyway, as a consequence of his geographical location, he tends to only get to West Country type games. Unfortunately this debacle was one of those games.

A week before we were due to go, I checked the train timetable and, based on this information, we planned our journey. We had a simple plan. I'd get a train from Waterloo to Dorchester South, Colin would drive down from Bridport, meet me about noon, leaving us three hours to travel the 90 or so miles to Plymouth. Sounds good on paper, but in the tradition of best laid plans of Millwall supporters and men, all did not go well . . .

I arrived at Waterloo well in time to catch the appropriate train, or so I thought. I learnt on arrival that the timetable had been changed that week and the train I wanted had already gone. No worries, I'll get the next one. I attempted to call Colin at home, only to find his local dialling code had changed. I usually called him at work, so I didn't know. I didn't have the new code, so never mind, I'll board the next train. I headed to my seat only to find myself next to a girl with a back-pack type of bag who made a big fuss about sitting in the correct seat, made an elaborate show of taking this back-pack off, bashing several people with it in the process, and once she eventually sat down, she decided she needed to get up several times for various reasons. Thankfully after a short "drama queen" style performance, she buggered off to pastures new.

The train proceeded at what seemed a tortuously slow pace only to stop completely a little way outside London. I sat wondering what was going on. Eventually it was announced that a car had crashed into a rail bridge further along the line, making it potentially dangerous to continue at anything more than a crawl.

By now, Colin had left Bridport. His wife Claire tried to call me on my mobile to check my progress. It was at this point that my 'phone decided to cut out. I couldn't call her back for reasons previously stated. Later on the signal was re-connected and I did actually speak to her. By this time both Colin and I were en-route so any chance of altering our plans were impossible.

Once we'd passed the damaged bridge, we carried on at a more normal speed. We did stop for quite a while at Poole harbour – very lovely and all that, but I was in no mood for sightseeing at this point. I eventually arrived at Dorchester South more than a little agitated and about an hour late. Colin was sitting in his car awaiting my arrival. He'd found out what the situation was so wasn't completely in the dark. That didn't help our plight, however, and we had a decision to make. Did we have enough time, two hours, to do the journey? Bearing in mind that most of the journey is on country roads, the motorway only coming into play at Exeter. If we didn't go, we had a couple of tempting alternatives. We could go shopping or we could go to see somebody like Lyme Regis or Winterton Abass play in the "Pal Marrowbone Jelly Division Five" or some such Mickey Mouse, or more Mickey Mouse, league.

We decided to give it a go and headed off at Michael Schumacher type speeds through the leafy country lanes in a race against time. Miraculously, and totally out of character to the way the day had so far gone (save for a couple of tractor related delays), we managed to reach Plymouth's outskirts with about five minutes to spare. As usual a town's football ground isn't sign-posted properly and in our haste we managed to take a wrong turn and found ourselves caught up in the town's one way system in a busy Saturday afternoon shopping area. Somehow we managed to negotiate this maze and found ourselves at Home Park. The ground is situated inside an actual park, which is uphill. We parked up where we could and ran to the ground - not easy considering our advancing years and my propensity for beer and eating. We reached the ground only to find the gate to the away end locked. Sweating, panting and beaten, we managed to attract the attention of a female steward, who after much persuasion and not to say begging, let us in in an act of Lady Di style mercy.

We'd got to the game half an hour late to witness a dour 0-0 draw, the only highlight of which was Millwall missing a penalty, obviously before we got there. Another perfect day, I'm sure you'll agree. Luckily I had the rest of the weekend in tranquil Bridport to soothe my shattered nerves. Beat that, Des Lynam.

CHAPTER 9

WINDSCREEN WIPER REPAIR SHOP

OVER THE YEARS I've been to away matches by most forms of transport - camel, pony and trap, and hovercraft being notable exceptions. My journeys by car have thrown up some memorable moments.

The main problem with travelling away, by car, apart from the motorway being a cone chicane, is trying to park when you get there and having to put up with being legally mugged at massively over-priced service stations en-route.

I've a theory that traffic wardens view football matches as their own personal Christmas club, while we poor unfortunates drive around and around a jungle of bollards, police no parking signs, double yellow lines, and permit holder zones, searching for the holy grail, or a legal parking space as it's known. I'm sure the wardens are hiding behind trees and such, giggling maniacally to see such fun, whilst awaiting the fatal slip that comes from desperation and leads to a ticket or – oh joy! – a clamping or towing away. Still despite this, we usually do actually manage to park, even if it does take us an hour to find a space. Strangely Jeremy Clarkson fails to mention this particular joy of motoring on *Top Gear* when he is trying to persuade us to buy some flash motor. Funny that.

The first time I went to a proper away match outside London, albeit not far outside, was when I went to Watford in 1970 with my cousins Roy and Nobby (don't ask), and Roy's mate Ronnie. We got lost and asked a local for directions. Our ears were attuned to Cockney speak and this man might as well have been from *The Archers* for all we could understand. We managed to find the ground, however, and wandered into the first stand we came to. This happened to be the "feared" Rookery End. No sign of the Brimson brothers sadly. No-one said a thing to us and we saw Millwall draw 1-1 thanks to a Gordon Bolland goal, my "first taste" of "life on the road" was "under my belt". I hope that's enough mixed metaphors for you.

The title of this chapter refers to a game I've mentioned in other chapters, the Chesterfield game in 1983, which was vital in Millwall not ending up "down among the dead men" or Rochdale as it's

53

known. We drove to this game, Steve Kimberley and I, in his Ford Granada, a fine car, but it didn't half make a racket over 60mph. It made the radio a bit of an unnecessary luxury, I can tell you. It was raining on the way up there and as is usual, the windscreen wiper broke at the most inopportune time. Fortunately the rain wasn't too bad and we made it to Chesterfield, looking for a motor spares shop. We asked a couple of locals if such a shop existed. They pointed to the only shop in the area, which, and I'm not making this up, was a windscreen wiper shop! If you're a Monty Python fan, you'll recognise this as a tale very similar to the cycling holidays bicycle pump repair shop sketch. It's true, honest.

In the 1980s Steve and I made the short trip to Brentford. We parked up in the first available spot, outside someone's house as it turned out. Upon returning to the car after the game, we found a sarcastic note telling us never to park there again, etc. What else was there to do other than write "bollocks" on the note and put it back from whence it came. Not polite, but to the point, I'm sure you'll agree.

Steve K and I also drove to Southampton for a second round League Cup replay at The Dell in October, 1985. We had drawn 0-0 at The Old Den and set off to The Dell to take up our position in the Rat Trap / Cage End or whatever it was actually called, not a treat for us. Claustrophobic's a bit OTT. Even Harry Houdini would have had a job escaping onto the pitch from this ground. The game itself ended 0-0 during normal time and we lost 5-4 on penalties. If memory serves, it was notable for an X Certificate display by John Fashanu and Joe Jordan, not a pretty sight, particularly if Joe didn't have his teeth in! We left the ground after our defeat and wandered around trying to locate our car. En-route we got trailed by a van load of blokes who, very fortunately for us, were Millwall, and once we identified ourselves they left for their locals man hunt. Another escape, thank God.

One of the more disastrous journeys was not solely a car journey, as we only drove to The Den to pick up the club coach, but it fits into this section due to the eventual chain of events. I went with Simon and two brothers, Paul and Nathan, my regular home and away companions for many recent years. Paul picked me up at Rotherhithe Tunnel and we headed off for The Den to pick up an early morning coach to Stockport for a Division Two game in January, 1997, a game we lost 5-1. We have the dubious distinction of appearing in a picture in *The Lion Roars* standing beneath a large scoreboard showing the score.

The journey up was pretty uneventful, so was the trip back to The Den. On arrival we found that the car headlights had been left on and we had a battery as dead as a dodo. We managed to push the car into the street immediately outside the ground, so that the gates could be locked. We called Paul and Nathan's dad, Dave. He is usually another regular away traveller, but for some reason he hadn't gone to this game. Just as well as it turned out, as he was able to come out with jump leads, etc. to try to get the car going. No joy, so we decided that as the area around the ground is not particularly well lit or salubrious, we should push the car to a better lit, busier street. As you can appreciate, the phrase "all we were short of" applies to this episode after an away coshing.

Paul, Nathan, Mad Ted, and I travelled to Brighton for a First Round League Cup tie at the beginning of the 2000-20001 season. We met up at Walthamstow and set off around the "road to hell" and across the Dartford Bridge. Very high, very long and very impressive it is too! We drove up the motorway and followed the directions on the leaflet which Brighton had provided with the tickets. It was entitled, "The Way To Withdean", and when I first saw it I thought it was a pamphlet from a cult offering spiritual enlightenment. But no, it was a detailed map basically showing that you couldn't park anywhere and should stop at a "park and ride" to be driven to the ground.

As this offer didn't start until 6.00pm and it was only 5.30pm when we arrived, we drove right up to the ground and tried to park in the car park there. No go unfortunately, so I said to Paul to have a drive around anyway, and miraculously we managed to get parked just across the road from the ground. We then set off in search of food, passing numerous "no football parking" signs in the posh area of Withdean. We walked for what seemed like miles until we found a Harvester pub, so we had a couple of pints and sampled the "soup in a basket" type fare.

Refuelled, we headed back to the ground, and what a peculiarity it was too. It was basically an athletic stadium (sic) with "Gerry" built temporary uncovered seating along one side and around the two corner sections behind one of the goals, but very little else save for someone's back garden at the other end and a stand that looked like a railway platform with a load of seats plonked on it along the other side.

Our stand consisted of 700 seats on a bouncy platform held up like a Meccano kit with sheets of plywood for added decoration. We scored twice and our celebrations gave me the impression that this rickety erection would give way at any minute. The fact that we were about ten miles from the pitch due to the running track, etc., only added to the bizarre spectacle.

We won 2-1, with Brighton scoring from a free-kick moved forward ten yards because of back chat - my first experience of this new rule. A couple of funny moments save for all the gay references I've already listed. The P.A. announcer said, "We have a small child in distress . . . " We naturally assumed he'd lost his parents, but no, he continued " . . . He's lost his sunglasses." Oh no! What a disaster.

The police also entered into the night's fun when walking past us four abreast around the running track. We all cheered for our favourite one to cross the finishing line first and egged them on as if it was an athletics event. Marvellous.

At the end of the game we were kept penned in behind the prison style fences for an inordinate amount of time, filmed by the police, and generally buggered about. To add insult to injury, they then opened the gates some way behind us, so we all had to turn around and walk back some distance just to get out. New season, usual old bollocks. We got back to the car to find it unclamped, unticketed, and not towed away. So two results in one night.

Simon, Dave and I drove to Oxford in the 1990s. Simon decided to take his young daughter Lisa with us. It was a very warm day, which didn't help, because the following scenario occurred. As we headed on to the motorway, Dave said to Simon "Is she alright in a car, she doesn't get sick does she?"

Simon turned to Lisa and said, "You're okay, you're not going to be sick are you?"

Lisa shook her head and with perfect timing threw up all over him. What with the heat and the smell, the trip to and from the ground was an unpleasant one, with the over-powering smell of vomit as our travelling companion. Lovely! We lost as well, if memory serves.

Dave has featured in most of the more amusing incidents at recent games away, for instance at Bristol Rovers in 1999. After losing 1-0 to a late, late strike, Dave, Paul, Nathan, Mad Ted and I headed back to the car. We'd stood on an open terrace in biting winds in a hailstorm, watched Millwall totally outplay the home team and lose. We headed back to the car freezing, soaked through, and not a bit pissed off. We got in the car and Dave decided he needed to relieve himself, which he did up against his own car in the main street outside. We sat in the car in some sort of perverse peep show as Dave did his business and offered a free view to the more noncey local yokels.

In the same season, we drove to Reading's Madejski stadium in a mini bus. We decided to park in the ground's car park. On arrival, Dave wound down the window and said to the attendant "I've not got £3, can I give you a wank instead?" The man laughed, but declined his kind offer saying he preferred cash. We do have to remind Dave to take money to games for parking, not rubber gloves and tissues.

He and Simon tend to think each town we visit is going to be suffering from a food shortage and so take enough food to feed an army. Dave also took a black plastic bag full to the brim with porno tapes to one away match, I know not why.

For a match on New Year's Day, 1985, Steve K and I went to Reading for a Division Three game that ended 2-2. We'd been out the night before on the usual New Year's Eve booze up, but still decided to go to the game even though it was a noon kick-off. Quite a few people in the away end were the worse for wear, some still in fancy dress presumably having come straight from a party. On the way back, Steve took his eyes off the road and shunted the car in front. In the exchange of details that followed, it transpired that the other owner's name was Moody. He was actually Mr Bad Moody on this day, as you can imagine.

Some away trips can be tragic. I've seen many crashes on the motorway including a jack-knifed lorry on the M1 and, on a trip to Middlesbrough, the road resembling a stock car race, and I've also seen air ambulances landing on the motorway to pick up the injured. Thankfully all of this has been from the safety of our car or coach. Considering the amount of games I've been driven to (I can't drive), I've only ever been involved in one dangerous incident.

Paul drove Nathan, Simon and I to Walsall in February 1997. We had a bit of trouble getting on to the motorway initially as we'd got a bit lost trying to find it from Chingford where the two brothers live. We eventually got on though and set off for our hundred mile or so trip. We'd left ourselves a good amount of time to do the journey – and thank God we had.

We were doing about 80 miles an hour in the middle lane when bang! – the car's white bonnet shot up and crashed into the windscreen, bending the wipers out of shape and forming a white wall blocking all forward vision. We continued on for a few moments while we tried to take in what had actually happened. Paul stopped the car in the middle lane and got out to see if he could put the bonnet down. It was bent completely out of shape and Paul couldn't do anything with it at all. All this, with cars flying past all around us. He got back into the car and fortunately we managed to get onto the hard shoulder.

As soon as we'd pulled in, a Range Rover pulled up behind us, driven by a local man (we weren't far from Walsall) who said he was amazed we'd made it this far without being killed. He said he'd called the police from his mobile and reported what he thought was a potentially fatal incident. He gave us a bungee rope to try and fix the bonnet down. We thanked him and tried to do something about the damage.

A couple of minutes later the police pulled up behind us in response to the call and even though we were in Millwall colours, they were very helpful. We got some more rope and they escorted us to a nearby service station to make sure the bonnet was now secure. They told us to drive in the slow lane/hard shoulder as much as possible and not to go too fast. We arrived at Walsall in good time, sat down and it was only then did we realise just how luck we were. What with this and Bobby Bowry scoring a 20 yard screamer, Millwall fans will understand the sheer shock of this alone. We managed to get home safely, if a bit slowly. We were beaten 2-1, but we were all just glad we were still alive.

CHAPTER 10

INDIANS ON THE HILLS

LET ME GIVE you a feel for what it's like to visit a town representing Millwall . . .

The townsfolk will view your arrival with the same trepidation they would reserve for Ghenghis Khan's hordes galloping up the High Street or Viking longboats sailing up the local river for a rape and pillage beano. They will tend to fortify their town accordingly, and so the usual order of the day is to board up your shops, shut all the pubs within a 20 mile radius, or hire several besuited gorillas to bounce on the door for the day.

They will gawp in wonderment at the away coaches with an expression they would usually display should a fleet of UFOs land on their front lawn. You will be filmed at every opportunity. There must be enough footage of me at away games to do my own version of *The Truman Show.* At some unscrupulous grounds you'll be overcharged "to cover extra policing costs" - obviously it's not because the home side are greedy bastards. You'll be body searched by a man with an evil grin and a rubber glove and you'll see more police than during the miners' strike, mass stewarding, police helicopters circling overhead, hoolivans, rabid police dogs, and police cavalry.

In some cases the police will forego their UN peacekeeping role and adopt a more pro-active role, i.e. cosh happy bonce bashing. I wouldn't have a bad word said about the police, they do a marvellous job. If this doesn't sound sarcastic, it should. Don't get me started.

Try this piece of "cod theorising" for size. The history of mankind is one of warring tribes and territories, each one having their own beliefs and "gods". This, to my mind, is the instinct that motivates football hooliganism, more than social conditioning. A bit high brow, but I went to a grammar school, so I am inherently posh. Ask anyone who knows me. It would explain why local rivalry is much more fierce than any other. To me, the 60s and 70s phenomenon of "end" taking was the equivalent of a raid on a rival village in years gone by.

There is also the north - south divide which has "Cockney" or London teams being seen in some sort of pampered privileged position in relation to their northern equivalent. Cheshire against

59

Newham – there, that's that one blown out of the water. It's all bollocks of course when you consider that areas such as Southwark and Tower Hamlets and many other inner city parts of London are always high on any social deprivation list. Still, it does give a focus for any hostility. We naturally play up this stereotype as my chants list shows, which doesn't go down too well for some reason.

England fly the flag fanwise in their own inimitable style and spread the hooligan ethos to the Continent, although I don't think the Italian Ultras, Dutch, Germans or Galatasaray need much schooling. Still it's tribal, although this time on a continental scale.

The Welsh don't like us much either as you will see later in this chapter. Crossing the Severn Bridge does give you the impression of entering holiday cottage burning bandit country.

Quite why Rugby Union doesn't get any trouble like football, I don't know. They probably see enough violence on the pitch to satisfy their blood lust and naturally they are more posh so prefer dropping their trousers, drinking yards of ale, and singing smutty ditties. Rugby League, well I would have said that they didn't have any trouble, then Hull went and wrecked Huddersfield. Anyway, I'm a soft southern softie, so I know nowt about Rugby League, happen.

There are hostile grounds and there are family clubs. Give me good old healthy hostility any day. You can't beat a bit of passion, not of the bodice ripping variety in this case, but a passionate "hot bed" crowd. It adds spice to a game for me anyway, as opposed to, say, family clubs!

Images of granny, Worther's Originals, the grandchildren, Christmas cardies and wicker hampers full of hot drinks and savoury treats, woolly mufflers and mittens in winter, all resplendent on a gingham table cloth with polite "Pass the cucumber sandwiches, Mater" banter. Eek! It chills my spine just writing it down. I'm not advocating outright hostility (oh yes I am!), but I'd rather save the polite applause for cricket and show jumping personally. But that's me I'm afraid.

As you will well know, Millwall most definitely come in the hostile ground category, along with Chelsea and West Ham in London, although Tottenham and Arsenal do have their moments. Most major cities have at least one nasty team – Birmingham City, Leicester City, Wolves, Stoke City, both Manchester clubs, Leeds Utd, Bristol City, Newcastle and Middlesbrough to name but a few. Sorry if I've left your club out, no offence.

However, when the perceived trouble club come to town, I can only speak for Millwall. There is a local "boys" turn out in the most unexpected of places. For example, at Scunthorpe the antics of the home fans was like watching a Desmond Morris documentary on Neanderthals and the missing link. And at Luton, Reading and Chesterfield we've been greeted by mouthy locals, - ill advised I'd have thought considering what's backing up the rhetoric. I wouldn't recommend them "larging" it at The Den. Still, sticks and stones and all that.

Although I've seen incidents of one degree or another nationwide, I thought I'd run through the more high profile or consistent trouble spots I've visited. Just to explain the title, it refers to my first visit to Newcastle, which has a chapter all to itself later on.

BRISTOL CITY: my first visit in 1984 came after a game at The Den where Bristol were followed around London, ambushed at a walky talky organised "off" and "run" in the ground. Me and Steve K headed to this game by car. We obviously didn't know the area, so we parked up near what we thought was the away end. We were wrong and had to walk all the way around the ground. As we approached the away end, we saw debris raining down onto our terrace. My first taste of down home West Country hospitality. We had the full body search and headed into the ground, sadly without crash helmets.

Millwall won 1-0 and the police, with Napoleonesque tactical nous decided the best policy would be to let everybody out at the same time in direct conflict with each other. Surprisingly it all went off in a Wild West style punch up in the park opposite the ground. How did that happen?

I've been to Bristol nine times to date and it's had an incident of one kind or another at all of these visits. One non-violent, but amusing incident was when we won 4-1 there. We were losing 1-0 at half time and the home fans to our left were rubbing our noses in it. We scored four in the second half, including a Teddy Sheringham hat-trick. This prompted a cessation in the verbals and a stand emptying out in midway through the second half quicker than a "on heat" skunks could have managed. So much for staying to the bitter end.

For this particular game we'd travelled on a special to Temple Meads and were herded on to buses for ferrying to the ground. Earlier coaches and buses had been ambushed and we were held some way away from the ground so the police could sort it out. When we did arrive, it was like driving into a human gauntlet with wall-to-wall Bristol fans surrounding the road. One bloke on our bus was urging everyone to have a go at the home fans when we got off. My theory: couple of buses of a few hundred versus home crowd of several thousand equals Custer's last stand, and he didn't do very well did he! So we declined his kind offer and made our way on battle alert into the ground. At one game, our coach was followed by a local who informed us, "You Cockneys are all mouth." Thanks, we always value an opinion.

STOKE CITY: We always get a warm Potteries welcome at Stoke. My first visit in 1993 was for a 2-1 win on the first game of the season. Simon and I went up on the club's special. The police met us outside the station and enquired obliquely if we'd like an escort to the ground as they had a few local "meatheads". We replied no thanks, we've got our own "meatheads" with us.

In the ground we stood on the terrace behind the goal with the Stoke "family" stand behind us and were berated by some old tosser who bore a striking similarity to Harry Enfield's "You don't want to do it like that" character. To our left we had a section of seats. Prior to the game Stoke tried to storm this section, met very stiff resistance and decided against it. After the game the police escorted us back to the station. As we approached the main road, we were met with a huge mob of Stoke coming from all angles. The police did their job in keeping the opposing factions apart and we arrived at Stoke station unscathed. A little while later, two bedraggled Millwall came into the station saying they'd gone into a local pub and been attacked and had their Millwall shirts ripped from them. Bearing in mind what the day had been like, I wouldn't have thought this idea was too sound to start with.

On the platform we had the privilege of the company of Lewisham's own Walter Mitty, Reg Burr. He, in true Billy Liar style, kept us all enthralled with his tales of financial wizardry (Tavern Holdings anyone? Now if he'd bought into Wetherspoons, we could have been millionaires, Rodney . . .) and his player and entertainment wheeler dealing acumen. It would have been quite amusing. I wish I'd have taped it. If it hadn't been so tragic.

More recently on a visit to the new Britannia Stadium, we sat behind the goal, dominated the game totally and lost 1-0 to a late, late goal. This prompted the home fans to come down to taunt us and to make motions to get on the pitch. Not ones to turn down an invitation, we tried to join them. The "off" was stopped by police and steward intervention. This quelled any major aggro, so naturally the best policy would be to let everyone out at once into the surrounding car park with only a wire mesh fence between us. Cue verbals and missile throwing, a Millwall surge to get at the home fans, which was halted by a large police v Millwall melee. Now I'm no military strategist, but couldn't this have been avoided by either diverting home fans away or by keeping us in the ground? But what do I know?

WOLVES: "Let's all have a disco!" Is this English? I've heard this song a lot at Wolves. A bit quaint, if you ask me, but local peculiarities aside, Wolves is always an adventure. I've been to Molineux many times and invariably seen trouble, rather like Bristol City.

Prior to the all-new improved stadium, Molineux was a dump. The away fans were penned in to the South Stand terrace next to what was the main bulk of Wolves "herberts". Thus to get back to the coaches or station meant going past the home opposition. The first couple of visits we were at least nearer to the station, but for future games, we were actually put in the other side of the stand and thus had to run the gauntlet back to the trains.

Wolves' policy seemed to be divide and conquer, whereby they would attack stragglers rather than confront the main bulk of the opposition's fans. This usually made for an interesting trip back to the station. I always survived a) because I'm a big lump and b) because you learn to be street wise. For one of my latter visits in the 90s, we sat in the new all seater South Stand. Once again nearer to the station everybody was let out together, so . . . outside of the ground is an underpass manned this day by local yobbos. The Police in a strategy of take the high ground were looking down from the road above. Good view, but little use should it go off. Well blow me it did. As soon as the cheery greeting "Come on Millwall, let's have it!" rent the air, one Wolves fan thought he'd try his luck, swung a punch at a bloke at the back, only for this man to knock him down flat. Bad luck, old boy. All to the amusement of the local constabulary.

As I said, it was always a good day to keep your wits about you, but by far the most frightening thing I saw at Wolves, save for The Beverley Sisters, was when we arrived early for a Saturday game, thought we'd have a wander about, had a look at the "Harrods" sized club shop and walked around to where the coaches came in. Our timing being perfect, we met our team's arrival. At this time Gavin Maguire played for us. Seeing this unshaven article, who bore a striking resemblance to Captain Scarlet's nemesis, Captain Black, in the flesh and up close was enough to scare the horses, I can tell you.

TOTTENHAM: In 1978 we played at Spurs in a Division Two game that ended 3-3. We were crammed into the Park Lane terrace. It was an excellent end to end game. The real adventures were outside the ground, however. Colin and I went to the game by overground from Liverpool Street. We walked up to the ground and were met by one rogue nutter who randomly struck out at anyone in range. Nothing to write home about really.

The journey back to Liverpool Street was much more eventful. We came out of the ground and walked up to White Hart Lane station. No sign of Tottenham whatsoever. The train was full of Millwall, but as they say in the old films, "It was quiet, too damned quiet". The train set off and Spurs' absence became apparent when on passing over any main road or railway bridge our journey became like something out of the North West frontier, as bricks and stones and other assorted debris rained down on us. Most of these bounced harmlessly off the roof. One, however, came through the window next to me and hit the occupant of that seat, fortunately on the body and not on the head. We'd opened the windows to allow this to happen as it seemed preferable to getting showered with glass.

On arrival at Liverpool Street, Colin and I got a bus back to the East End and Millwall were marched back on foot across the Thames. This station also saw a confrontation with West Ham on the return journey from our Division One relegation day at Ipswich in 1996, when "The Happy Hammers" very kindly turned up to take the piss. Cheers.

MAN UTD: In our two seasons in the top flight, as they say, we had two away trips to Old Trafford. At this time the Stretford End was still a covered "Kop" like terrace and we were packed into a terrace directly opposite this and beneath the home fans seating. My visits were both by Millwall Club Specials, the second of which arrived about ten minutes before kick-off and meant a double time route march to the ground to arrive seconds before kick-off. Both journeys terminated at Warwick Road, having passed up the side of the Lancashire County Cricket Ground. For both games we had our full allocation of about 4,000. We made a lot of noise, but were completely surrounded by Mancs, or wherever they came from.

Fighting broke out in the seats to our left at both games. It was a bit oppressive, a bit like being John Wayne at The Alamo. I didn't know Simon at this time, but he travelled up to one of the games via Manchester itself and got battered in the town centre, ending up at the game in plaster.

After both games, two defeats, we were kept in the ground while the smug bastard masquerading as an announcer / DJ repeated the match score to us. Cheers. We were eventually frog-marched to the station where, for the first game at least, we were held again for bloody hours while horses dribbled all over us and trod on our feet. Lovely.

We were warned to pull the train blinds down to offer some protection should we get bricked. We did, but we didn't. These two matches had been the first time we'd played Man Utd since 1974/5. That season for The Old Den game the press went to town completely, as Man Utd had a very bad reputation at the time and a visit to Millwall, well, it goes without saying. The stories in the press prior to the night match in September, 1974, read like a penny dreadful, with the railway arches and side streets around The Old Den being described as something straight out of Jack The Ripper era Whitechapel. "Rivers of blood, death on the streets, and other such tosh. The papers must have been very miffed when the game, a 1-0 defeat, ended without incident due to the total absence of any Man Utd fans, whose trains had been turned back apparently.

The worst violence I've ever seen at a football ground, inside anyway, was when my Dad took me to West Ham to see Man Utd win the title in the late 60s. They beat West Ham 6-1 and the game was notable for the toilet roll strewn goal mouths, a steady procession of ejections from the crowd, and bottle and dart throwing (an old favourite), resulting in a stream of bloodied casualties with head wounds. And I thought we were the only violent fans!

PORTSMOUTH: One of our more consistent enemies in the 70s and 80s were Portsmouth with pitched battles home and away, and I recall one game at The Old Den when smoke bombs were hurled at the away fans. These sort of incidents led to away fan bans and the like. Millwall actually played some games at Fratton, when we had one of our ground closures, so whether this started the ill feeling, I don't know. I'm sure it didn't help.

I've never actually encountered any problems myself at Pompey, but I have heard of the old brick lobbing attacks on the open away end from various mates. I did walk into a couple of "specials" of

Portsmouth coming out of New Cross Gate station for one game in the 80s. I'd got a train to New Cross for this particular game and was walking up to the ground past New Cross Gate station when I walked slap bang into a great mob of Pompey being escorted to the ground. The route to The Old Den from this station was through residential streets and you could usually hear the tannoy announcements and the home crowd noise as you walked to the game. For this particular match I could sense the away fans' tension. Being in the bloody middle of them, I didn't need to be telepathic. As we neared the ground I could hear the sounds of battle - lovely, and me in the midst of the enemy. I managed to get safely to the ground, flashed my Millwall season ticket and nipped past the police cordon. Home at last thankfully!

LUTON TOWN: I've been to Luton about a dozen times, excluding my one trip with some Tottenham mates to witness Ardiles and Villa's return to English football after the Falklands War. I can only remember one defeat and that was the famous 1-0 FA Cup quarter final, but that's selective memory for you. TV's stock footage riot night. Don't get me started, see Chapter 13 instead!

Colin and I went to Luton with a brother of another friend of ours for a game in 1972. We drew 2-2. Colin, Peter Webb and I had gone to the game via train. After the game we headed back to the station and got accosted by a gang of Luton fans who demanded one of our scarves. After an altercation we gave in due to being outnumbered, and they left us in peace. We met up with more Millwall on the way back to the station who said they were going on a home fan hunt and would get them for us.

We walked back to the train over a footbridge and arrived to wait for our train. Whilst standing reading the programme the local police tried to collar Colin for beating up someone on the bridge, which they claimed to have witnessed. For your information, Colin's a very mild mannered chap who at the time bore a striking resemblance to Mark Lester in *Oliver*, curly hair and innocent face sort of thing, plus he also had glasses on and a parka, your archetypal football hooligan if ever I've seen one. After further discussions we somehow managed to talk the Old Bill out of their "fit up" ideas and boarded our London bound train.

OXFORD: I've heard some strange things said at football to me / us at away matches, but a game at Oxford in the 90s took the award for stupidity. I went to the game with Micky on a City Express bus from

Aldgate in the City of London, to practically outside the ground. We got off the bus and went into the nearest pub, saw the game, and met up with some mates who'd travelled up on the train. We decided to go back with them on the train.

The walk back to Oxford station is what we in the trade call "bloody miles". On the way we were flanked by police and followed by young Oxford "boys". Picture the scene: I'm 16 stone, Micky's six foot plus and about 20 stone, and we've got police all around us. It was at this time that Oxford's "top" boy says to us, "The police are here Millwall, let's have it!"

I was too confused to react. Think of the logic of the situation and of this sentence. The combined weight of Micky and me was about three times his and if we'd punched our weight, he would have flown cartoon style about ten feet up in the air. Also, the thought that the most opportune time for a punch up is with a police escort would lead me to the conclusion that this genius didn't come from the academic quarter of town.

We eventually reached the station and got a train back to Paddington, with only our bus tickets for company. Naturally "sod's law" being what it is, a ticket collector appeared. Micky said, "The police told us to get on the train, mate." Amazingly this ploy worked and we got a free ride home.

On an earlier trip to Oxford, Steve K and I parked in a side street some way from the ground. After the game we got back to the car, sat down and watched a mob of Oxford charge up the road in our direction. As they raced past, we saw they were being chased by two or three Millwall fans. Isn't reputation a marvellous thing?

DERBY: As a pre-script to the Derby play-off riot game at The New Den, we played the first leg at the Baseball Ground and lost 2-0. We were spat on all afternoon from the stand above us and abused by morons on the way out. I did point out to one particularly mouthy local that it might be just a smidge more hostile for the away return than he'd like. Not quite this politely – more old fish wife industrial language I'm afraid. Sorry. The words were to prove prophetic.

As you may know, Derby were shown rioting and rampaging around the pitch at Southend shortly before our game. This was shown on a Friday night London current affairs programme, but strangely this wasn't mentioned in quite the same hysterical fashion as our actions during and after the return leg. Funny that.

On my return home after the first game, my day actually got worse, adding injury to insult as it were. I arrived back at The Den by coach, andDave dropped me off at a pub in Bethnal Green where I'd arranged to meet two of my non-football mates, Keith and Steve. When I got there, a bit late, I was surprised to find they'd not arrived. I ordered a pint and was less than half way through it when they walked in, Steve with blood pouring out of a wound by is temple. He'd been shot in the head by an air rifle en route to the pub. We left straight away and got a cab to the casualty at The Royal London Hospital where, as is usual, we had to sit for four hours before they could extract the pellet, which was quite well embedded. I eventually got home well after 1.00am in the morning. "Good day at the office?" No it bloody wasn't!

The home leg started for us at Whitechapel's East London line, when it was announced that clashes at Surrey Quays (docks!) had shut the station. We therefore got to the ground quite late and had to sit in the back of the South Stand in the nose bleed vertigo section. The game featured some pitch invasions, mostly due to piss poor policing and stewarding, with players being attacked and racially abused. Paul Williams deserved all he got as he kicked anything that moved in a petulant display. Still he can kick who he wants and get away with it and when we insult him because of this behaviour, we're seen as the real villains. I thought "sticks and stones (and kicking lumps out of all and sundry) may break my bones, but words will never hurt me." Obviously in PC World (our society, not the computershop) violent behaviour is more acceptable than verbal abuse. What a strange, cock-eyed concept.

It was said that the pitch invasions were an attempt to attack the away fans sitting in the upper tier. It's reality check time; to do this, certain options would apply. Let me run these by you and see how likely an attack inside the ground would be:

Option 1: You would need to climb a small wall, run up the lower tier, down on to the concourse then upstairs and straight into the opposition masses. I think the element of surprise may not be on your side somehow. Perhaps if you were Jackie Chan or Mike Tyson, you might pull it off successfully.

Option 2: Follow initial steps as Option 1, but scale wall between lower and upper tiers and again find yourself head long into the path of away masses. This time, I think grappling hooks, crampons and Batman's utility belt might be useful. Once again, no element of surprise. Perhaps if you were Chris Bonnington or the SAS, you might fancy your chances. The Milk Tray man might just pull it off also.

Perhaps if you think these two options are viable, you could be just the man for the new James Bond, once old Pierce Brosnan packs it in. Dave did, however, get his car smashed up in the car park in the disturbances outside after the game. He got compensation from the club, as he worked for Millwall's Executive Club at the time.

BIRMINGHAM: My first "real" away match outside the London region. My attitude at away matches or at home for that matter, is if attacked, fight. I'm not going to instigate anything, but I'm not going to be someone's punch bag, that's an absolute certainty. As a consequence, I've never actually been physically attacked apart from at Birmingham in 1972 as a 13 year old boy. My Dad told me not to go, but I knew better, of course, as you do at that age. It proved to be a very eventful day all around.

I went to this game with Colin, another school mate, Paul White, and Paul's cousin, who was down from Swindon. The four of us arrived at Euston at about 9.00am. We bought our return tickets and set about playing cards until the train was due. At this time I was dressing like a "skinhead", although my curly hair made me more like Harpo Marx. Still, I had a white Levi's jacket, Doc Marten boots and a very stylish, I thought, trilby hat. We were messing about and I naturally thought the safest place to keep my ticket was in the hat band of my trilby, which then got tossed about in usual teenage boy style horseplay. Well this may surprise you, but I lost my ticket and as the train was due to go any minute we decided that my mates should go and I'd try to get a later train.

I got another train ticket and although a bit distraught and not to say skint, I managed to get the next train up. This was full of adults who all seemed to be drunk, each carriage and compartment clinking with the sounds of empty beer cans. We arrived at New Street and the first thought was to confront any waiting Birmingham. As we got off the train, we all began to sing "Fuck off Birmingham, I said fuck off Birmingham!" to the tune of Ringo Starr's hit at the time, *Back Off Boogaloo*. Any Brummies that were there scarpered and we set off outside the station, where we were all stopped and searched by the police, the result of which was enough "cutlery" to equip any kitchen.

Our next port of call was a quick rampage through The Bullring shopping centre, boxes flying, stalls knocked over, shoppers fleeing. You know the sort of thing. Our original throng was progressively being thinned out as people went into shops, cafes, and pubs, but I decided my best bet was to head to the ground in a vain attempt to find my mates. No easy task in a 43,000 crowd who had assembled for this vital old Division Two promotion battle.

I forgot to mention some accessories that set off my ensemble that day. It was a fashion at the time to have scarves tied around your wrist a la Bay City Rollers. Come to think of it, we must have looked like complete prats, but who knew? I had two silk Millwall scarves on, one on each wrist. By the time I got close to the ground, it was apparent that I was more or less alone. As we passed a local pub, the "boys" outside pointed in my direction. One of their number, a six foot black bloke, came across the road towards me and uttered the immortal words "Got the time, mate?" in his best Jasper Carrott accent.

I replied in my best Arthur Mullard, "Yeah, it's one o'clock, mate."

He then proceeded to rain blows on me, very heroic considering I was only a kid at the time. I can honestly say I didn't feel anything, pain wise. Just goes to show what a wanker the bloke was I suppose.

I carried on to the ground. I didn't have enough money to get a programme and barely enough to get into the ground. I followed some 100 or so fellow Millwall into a section to the left of the covered shed end of the ground. I subsequently discovered that this was the home end. I seem to recall a large-ish empty space around us, but we went the whole game unapproached. We lost 1-0 to an extremely dodgy goal. I headed into the street and I was contemplating how nice the walk back from Euston would be, when amazingly I bumped into my mates and managed to cadge the fare money for my tube ticket.

There have been several other Birmingham incidents since. I recall two Brummies being stretchered out of The New Den's West Stand, one with a broken collar bone after getting battered in a game in the 90s. Still I thought common sense would dictate sitting in the home stand at Millwall might be unwise. Another example of the usual state of play at Birmingham was for a night match in 1993, when our fans mugged the programme sellers and our own fans almost attacked those of us who came by coach thinking we were Brummies.

Unfortunately, I couldn't get to the infamous 2-2 game in the 1990s, but I've had several good reliable reports about the whole shambles. The phrase "accident waiting to happen" springs to mind for some reason. Karen Brady might be attractive and a great female role model, but she's obviously got a very rose coloured, head in the sand view of her own fans, and a chief steward or

70

security advisor that I wouldn't trust as a lollipop man on a school crossing. I might be a bit cynical, but who caused all the trouble against Leeds a few seasons back and had running battles with Wolves in 1999 / 2000, or was that our fault as well? Replies on a postcard, please.

It was for the return "bout" to this first game that I got thumped by a riot copper outside the ground while waiting to wave the away fans off. How was I to know? I thought all the medieval armour and cavalry charges were a re-enactment of some Middle Ages battle, an easy mistake to make.

The phrase "disaster waiting to happen" can certainly be used for the two most notorious away clashes involving Millwall in the last two seasons. Now call me a tactically naïve cynic, but is there some higher logic at work that I'm at a loss to understand or are the security organisers behind these type of events simply idiots?

We played in South Wales at Swansea for a glorious 3-0 Friday night FA Cup First Round defeat. At this game I think I can safely say, without fear of contradiction, that the locals were more than up for it, leading to riot police outside stopping a more "hands-on" welcome. Now add this to the fact that for a midweek First Round Auto Windscreen game at The Den, a nothing game at the time, Cardiff brought down a couple of hundred "meatheads" who were "right tuned up for it" as we say.

To me these two events might lead to the conclusion that games against South Welsh opposition might be a bit volatile, but to my mind the two words "football" and "intelligence" do not make good bedfellows. In fact you could say that they are sleeping in separate beds, if not rooms, if you understand my ramblings.

The same can certainly be said about the high profile game at Maine Road in 1999. This game followed a particularly hostile night at The Den, and in my experience, if you threaten Millwall on the internet or by carrier pigeon for that matter, the usual response is for a bigger away presence, not a smaller one, so my theory of security organisation as listed previously would still hold true. But what do I know. Reports from the front . . .

MANCHESTER CITY: I've been to Maine Road three times, twice in the space of eight days in our last season in the top Division, one League game and one Cup game. On the coach to the ground it dawned on me what a lovely area Moss Side was and that the locals had a "Wolvesesque" divide and conquer, straggler attacking policy.

So add this to what I've just said and I thought it might just go "off" at our game a couple of seasons ago, and do you know I was right.

At Maine Road the stage was beautifully set for mayhem. Picture the scene: the game at The New Den was played out in a "bear pit" atmosphere. Millwall had two goals disallowed, both sides had a man sent off after a mass brawl, Man City "got out of jail" with a late, late goal, prompting Joe Royle's usual old cobblers. Remember to engage brain, then talk, I think it may help. Just a tip. And finally a full scale police v Lions fans riot outside the ground after the game.

So you're planning the away leg security. What do you do? Mmmm! Let me see . . . Make the game all ticket, give Millwall the whole of one end - as Millwall always do at home irrespective of whether the away turn out is four or 4,000, and insist that all away fans travel on designated transport, either coaches or trains, but not both, as this would mean spreading your resources too thin. If it's by coach, pick the coaches up on the motorway and escort them en masse to the ground. Once emptied, put coaches in a secure area guarded for the whole game until they are boarded at the final whistle and then escort them out of Manchester.

Poppycock! This is how you handle it . . . You do make it all ticket, well done! But you give Millwall a section in the corner leaving only six rows of seats between away and home fans. You leave the coaches unescorted to make their own way through one of England's most notorious areas and then come up with some cock and bull excuse. You park the away coaches outside the Kippax unguarded, you allow Man City to practically double the ticket costs to away fans to cover policing, and then very logically you keep the away section bar open until kick-off time - take kick-off whichever way you wish. It's patently obvious that a pissed-up fan is more controllable, everyone knows that. For the icing on the cake, you permit Joe Royle to put inflammatory revenge type verbiage into the match day programme. Obviously if you were there or a Millwall fan, in general you'd know this, but just in case you don't, I thought I'd spell it out.

Now you don't have to be Napoleon to organise this, as I've told you can do and I'm not Napoleon, although I do share a birthday (day and month, not year!). So maybe you do, but I think getting the Three Stooges and The Keystone Cops in wasn't advisable either.

My day started at The New Den early Saturday morning when we boarded one of the 20 or so coaches that went up that day. We moved convoy style up the motorway and headed unescorted into

Moss Side. We saw no police and, more surprisingly, no Man City. We were all honestly expecting an ambush. But no.

I went to this game with Simon, his son Patrick, who was about seven at the time, Dave, Paul and Nathan. We arrived reasonably early and contrary to a great Millwall away tradition, we decided to sit in the correct seats. Our six seats were in the front row of the upper tier with a no-mans land in front of us. As we sat down, I was furthest from a stairway aisle and about half a dozen empty seats away from an aisle gap and next to what at the time was an empty stand. A steward was close by and we started to talk to him. He announced himself as the chief steward, and, it became apparent, Britain's only surviving brain donor. It became obvious to us that if this arrogant prick had organised the day, we were in trouble.

Dave said to him, "Who's in the section next to us?"

"Oh! That's Man City fans", he cheerfully replied. "It's okay though, they're juniors and family members."

We looked at each other and decided on our defence plans. We moved Patrick to a safe position. We realised that if an attack was coming, this was where it was coming from. We decided a "hold your ground - fight where you stand" policy was best. I was closest and as I'm the biggest, it seemed logical. Paul and Nathan are black belts in karate and I did it for three years. Simon did boxing so I think we might just be able to cope.

We pointed out to this clueless prat the flaws in his masterplan and were given assurances based purely on ignorance and arrogance on his part. We, however, live in the real world and knew better. Sure enough, come three o'clock, the block next to us was "meathead heaven" and the only family at home here would be of the Manson variety.

We stood for the whole game facing each other with abuse and coins flying in equal measure. I got hit in the face with coins and told Patrick to pick up any money he found on the ground. A police officer standing in front of me was telling Millwall supporters to shut up and not to abuse City fans. I pointed out to this officer that if he cared to look, he'd see both sets of fans were doing the same thing, so why wasn't he berating them? This was met by the usual "might as well talk to the wall" situation. I carried on my argument, but Simon said to me, "I'd shut up if I were you or he'll nick you".

I took notice of what he said as he was probably right, but it's wrong that even-handed treatment isn't the order of the day in these situations. Much to my surprise apart from a few Lee Van Cleef style stares, no frontal assaults were forthcoming. In the second half, seating was thrown to accompany the coins and Millwall surged towards the City fans. Cue the riot police who waded into us and only us indiscriminately. I saw one innocent bystander get knocked over a wall and continually clubbed for his trouble. Amazingly, City got none of this hospitality.

The tannoy system told Man City fans not to get involved. No need anyway as the Old Bill were doing their job for them. We lost 3-0 and were kept in the ground for about an hour. The police and tannoy told us this was for our own safety. Bearing in mind what had happened on the day, I'd say we had more to worry about from the boys in blue in front of us than the boys in sky blue outside. It did, however, give Man City fans sufficient time to smash up our coaches to the tune of £24,000 worth of damage and to hospitalise one poor coach driver.

We boarded the coaches and set off, again unescorted back to London. We told Patrick and another small boy he was sitting with to stay near the toilet so they could get inside if we were attacked. When it escalated in the ground, Simon took Patrick down to the front out of the way, and he managed to pick up some the money that had rained down on us.

I said to him "Were you frightened?"

He said "No, but I've got over a pound in change!"

The steward at the front told Simon that the organisation for this game was totally different to usual policy. In fact, it was normally much better segregated and less money for other teams. The next day in the Sunday paper the media went to town, implying that we wrecked our own coaches, hospitalised one of our own drivers, etc. If we had, it must have been by way of *Carrie*-like telekinesis as we were locked in the ground at the time. We did all manage to appear in the *News Of The World* and *The Daily Mail* on Monday, the images showing the riot police wading into our section. "Can I have a 12" x 10" blow up, please?"

CARDIFF: Several years ago we had the misfortune of following several Cardiff coaches on Commercial Road, in the East End, on their way home from West Ham. We were in a car on our way home from an event on the Isle Of Dogs. What we saw was the car in front have a coach window pushed on to it from the inhabitants of the coach. Very sensible, I'm sure, and not a bit windy.

I only mention this to show what type of mentality they have. At games previously there had been trouble between us and them, so everyone knew what the likely outcome of any game was going to be.

Like every other supporter, the first sight of a new season's fixtures is always an important event. Imagine my surprise, not to say shock, first game of the 1999/2000 season, Cardiff away. Are they mad? We all thought, if they had sense this game – a cast iron certainty trouble game would be buried in mid-season on a midweek night and likewise for the London bout. Still I'm not Chip Millibert or whatever his name is, so what do I know?

In line with my paranoid conspiracy theory, you again have two options:

a) Are the League and police stupid?

b) Or do they want it to happen?

It has been mooted in Millwall's fanzines that perhaps the idea was to get the volatile games out of the way before our World Cup bid became due. This is quite possible, I'd have thought.

Anyway, we went to the game on the club coaches again, with Simon, Patrick, Dave, Paul and Nathan. The journey up was uneventful. We told Patrick that we were leaving England as we crossed the Severn Bridge. He was getting worried that he wouldn't be let back into our country. Again, we adopted the toilet shelter policy for the kids.

Just to make it more interesting, the day of the match coincided with a town gala or some such. This added to the chaos. The coaches picked up the escort outside Cardiff, and bizarrely, we were d'iven right through the city centre and past the Millennium Stadium – there's posh for you – and more importantly, past all the pubs, which we did at a snail's pace. We had "boys" following us on foot, "giving it large" all the way. We drove past a side street near to the ground which the police had road blocked and manned with a large riot police presence with the customary helicopter circling above. The kick-off was approaching, but the police took us into a siding by an industrial estate away from the ground. We were kept there until about 3.15 pm, the police telling us that it was to clear home fans away and that the match would be delayed accordingly. Yeah, right! So we arrive at the ground only to find we'd missed half of the first half obviously. It was a bit lively in the ground and as we stood on the sun baked open terrace, we looked across at what we thought was a covered terrace on our right, only to find that it was in fact a seated stand with all its occupants standing up.

There was the usual exchange of pleasantries with anti English chants and claims on Cardiff's part of victories earlier in the day.

Whether this was true, I couldn't say, as I'd not personally seen any combat. However, some weeks later we went to Colchester. Waiting on the platform on the way home some London police officers started talking to us. They usually travel with Millwall to away games. One of them told us what he'd seen and that was 11 Millwall attacked by about 300 Cardiff. Good odds. He said he thought that they were all going to die, police included. If this is the idea of what constitutes a victory, you can stuff it.

Back in the ground, Millwall scored from a Neil Harris penalty and we moved along the terrace towards the Cardiff. Cue surge from home seats, collision being avoided by the police. Cardiff then got a penalty at our end of the ground, only for the taker to get pelted with plastic Coca-Cola bottles. He scored and made it 1-1. Tony Warner, Millwall's goalkeeper, was later charged and acquitted of injuring a home fan with a similar bottle.

The game ended in a draw and the police kept us behind on the open terrace and then let the Cardiff fans in behind this terrace. Cue missile attacks as debris rained down on us. I suggested we get closer to the back wall for safety. The stewards then opened the gates on to the pitch and we moved out of range of the police instigated "duck shoot" that was the away terrace.

Several people had head injuries from missiles. We walked on to the pitch fuming at the stupidity of letting home fans into this position. An outside gate was opened on to the terrace and skirmishes broke out. Nothing major ensued, though. One Millwall fan started booting the dug-out in rage and picked up a fire extinguisher. This was taken from him and later turned on us by a steward, trying to stop people, children mostly, from entering the players tunnel. What this idiot didn't realise was that these people had been told to seek refuge here by the police.

Simon and Patrick actually went into the players' dressing room. I tried to get outside via the main stand exits, along with several others, but some of our number were battered by riot police and streaming with blood, came back onto the pitch.

We stood around awaiting our exit and surveying the scene, I saw many people with head wounds. One man I saw had a "V" shaped indentation in his head from a brick, others had riot police inflicted wounds.

There were London police there, as I mentioned. We asked them what idiot had decided police strategy and whether it had been logical. They couldn't answer, but their general manner was that it had been badly organised, "piss-up in a brewery" style.

We did eventually get outside and it was deserted. We found damage to some of the coaches and "Millwall scum" printed on an outside wall in lurid coloured paint. We boarded the coaches, turned out of the car park and found ourselves more or less on the motorway. Why didn't we come in this way?

You've got to ask why the police decided to take us through the city centre - thus increasing, not decreasing the risk of ambush, I would have thought.

As you can imagine, the Teletext on Saturday and the Sunday scandal sheets had a field day about this game. They spoke of internet organised "off of the decade" type of stuff. I don't know if this was true, I have trouble operating a calculator, but it does let the sensationalist press add a high tech and more sinister dimension to the day's proceedings.

Naturally, cue paranoia, the TV footage I saw was nearly all of us in the ground and on the pitch and trying to get out via the main stand. Apart from a few shots of Cardiff being moved on in the streets by riot police, it was all us. No sign of Cardiff's missile throwing and general mayhem outside. Perhaps Kate Adie was unavailable that day? One thing that does irk me (only one?) is the total lack of accuracy of the reporting. Quite how you're supposed to believe anything the media says, when what you witness yourself is falsely reported, I don't know. In this case, as soon as we got on the coach, the radio informed us that we'd invaded the pitch. News to us. I suppose "The stewards opened the pitch gates to allow the away fans to avoid being bombarded due to police incompetence," isn't sensational enough. Still, "Sod the facts, let's print / broadcast it."

CHAPTER 11

"FAR HAWAY THE LADS!"

AT THE END of our first season in Division One (now the Premiership), we had a game against a relegation threatened Newcastle at St. James's Park. I went to this game with two brothers, Micky and Steve Fisher. Micky who I've already mentioned in dispatches, had a Geordie friend Bob, who worked in the East End. He was going up to Newcastle for this weekend to visit his wife, so we planned to meet up with him there. The plan was that Steve and I would catch a National Bus on the Friday and arrive late afternoon. We were to stay at a guest house for the weekend, which Bob had booked up for us. Nice place, £10 a fortnight. Steve and I left Victoria Coach Station late morning, with Micky due to get an overnight "pisshead" special late Friday night. He was to stay with Bob and his wife.

We sat on the upper deck of the bus in boiling conditions, we got stuck on the motorway and the air conditioning didn't work. This delay was due to a lorry jack-knifing in front of us and meant we were held up for a couple of hours. We'd arranged for Bob to meet us at the bus station and naturally our late arrival meant he'd been waiting for ages when we eventually arrived.

The idea was that he'd show us a few decent pubs for the evening. As we were late and he had plans for the night, this tour was done at break-neck and not to say "down your neck" speed. We had about five pints in five different bars in about half an hour.

Bob showed us to our guest house and gave us a couple of tips: "Stay off the Newcastle Exhibition" or "E" as it's known, and "Don't ask pub barmaids to get you a cab as you do in London as it's not done here."

"Okay", we said.

Steve and I went to our separate rooms and he proceeded to sing Bee Gees songs at the top of his voice. Did I mention he's a bit mad? He used to chat girls up in clubs by telling them he was "The greatest swordsman in all France" or asking them if they wanted to come home with him as he had "a suckling pig on the spit" indoors. Miraculously this worked on numerous occasions!

He came into my room whilst I was resplendent in my underpants and announced that I looked like a slimmer version of his brother. Strange but true.

We headed out for the night via a local chip shop staffed by Geordie speaking Indians. A bizarre combination, I thought, but that's me. We went to a pub nearby and replenished our falling alcohol levels. We decided to head to the main part of town for the night, so we called a cab from the 'phone on the bar. Strangely, they couldn't understand a word we were saying, so contrary to Bob's instructions, we had to ask the barmaid to get us a cab. We communicated our intentions by means of Pidgin English - "Men they go club" sort of thing.

We managed to get a cab and set off for the bright lights of Newcastle. If you've not been to Newcastle, it's good clean fun, chock full of bars, clubs, and semi-naked northern girls. Marvellous. We did a bit of a crawl around the bars we'd been introduced to earlier and we got talking to some local girls who were mesmerised by our Cockney charm and wide boys from the Smoke wit. They were fascinated by the way we said "South" or "Sarf", or to give it its full title, "Dahn Sarf". Sounds like a Thai dish I once had, now I come to think of it, but I digress. They kept asking us to repeat it over and over again. Still, simple things and all that. We said we were going on to a club and did they want to join us. They said they had to work next morning, why didn't we visit them then? At Dolcis, I think. We said "Okay" and set off to The Mayfair Club, a venue made famous years later by Paul Gascoigne's antics.

We carried on drinking and by this time, Steve was lagging a bit and spent most of the time in the club hanging on to a post. We left the club and decided it was an excellent time to have an Indian, i.e. we were plastered. We wandered around and found a back street curry house. Now we're from the East End, so we know a curry house when we see one and this one was a khazi. We sat down, looked around and loudly exclaimed "What a shithole!" and walked out.

We then meandered around the streets for a while and came upon a curry house which in our stupor we didn't recognise. Little did we know in our self inflicted condition that it was the same one we'd reviewed previously, so upon entry they promptly threw us out.

We went back to our guest house and went to bed. At about 10.00 am the next morning, we sheepishly crept down to the dining room and had the "Full English" - like the "Full Monty", but you keep your clothes on!

Bob rang to say he was coming around to pick us up. He arrived with his brother Maurice and drove us down to Warbottle, where he and his wife lived. We went into their house, said our "Hello's", and Steve threw up in the upstairs toilet.

As it was about 10.30am, we thought it high time we had another drink. You know what it's like on your holidays? So we headed for the local pub, The Engine. It was a real old fashioned type of pub with a pool table being the main point of interest. By this time Micky had joined us and I started to drink "E" against Doctor Bob's instructions.

The locals, headed by Wor Jacko, who was about a hundred, mumbled about having Cockneys in their pub, taking over the pool table, which we had, but given our combined weight and size, they doubted the wisdom of challenging us, saying "Would you look at the size of the buggers!"

They moaned about Sunderland and commented that we, as London's ambassadors, swore much more than Geordies did, a bit rich when you consider that Chubby Brown comes from this general neck of the woods and his language would make a docker blush. What I did notice was that in the presence of such a strong accent as Geordie, we got more Cockney, much more "Cor Blimey Governor, cor love a duck, knock it on the head, boiled beef and carrots". You get my drift, in a sort of Dick Van Dyke in *Mary Poppins* stylee.

The "E" was going down very well, a bit too well in truth and we stayed in The Engine until about 2pm, when we got a cab up to the ground. He dropped us off by the away end, where we saw a few bloodied casualties who'd encountered bother from the locals when heavily outnumbered in the nearby pubs.

A policeman outside the ground asked if we'd been drinking. "No" we said. No, but I wouldn't light a match near my breath if I were you. Not unless you like singed eyebrows anyway.

We stood on an open terrace at the opposite end to the Gallowgate End. At this time both ends were open terraces, more park bench than debenture and not the palatial splendour it is now. Newcastle were second from bottom at the time and were a bit miffed that their hero, Mirandinha, was not playing. He got more response in the grandstand to our right than the team did on the pitch.

Teddy Sheringham scored a blinding goal at the precise moment that Steve chose to go the burger stall, so he went 250 miles only to miss Millwall's high point of the afternoon. The Geordies equalised with an equally spectacular effort, but the whole game was punctuated with "Sack the Board!" chants. It's good to see that more than ten years on, nothing changes.

At the end of the game, the Gallowgate end sat down en masse and had a "sit-in" protest. I believe they had to win to stay up or were in fact already down, I'm not sure. The few hundred of us there decided it would be polite to help out the locals with their "Sack the Board" chants, so we did.

After quite a while, the police let us out and escorted us back to Newcastle station. They advised us not to go into the town that night, as a relegated team does not a happy fan make. On the way back the Geordies followed us up the side streets. This reminded me of the old Westerns where the cavalry spot the Indians tracking them from the hills, hence the earlier chapter title. We arrived back at the station knowing it would go off. It did to a degree.

However, the only reason we went back to the station was because the police took us there and we headed for the cab rank in order to get back to Warbottle to join up for a night out with Bob and his wife. We got a mini cab outside the station. The driver was barking mad, looked like Jackie Charlton, flat cap and all, and for some reason thought we were Geordies, an easy mistake to make. We went back to The Engine to continue our drinking activities. After a while we went to a decidedly greasy chip shop and then back to Bob's wife's house where we ate our chips, etc whilst watching the Eurovision Song Contest on TV. Now if that's not God's way of telling you to get back to the pub, I don't know what is!

Bob and his wife joined us at a more upmarket local pub, where he acted as an interpreter, he being fluent in Geordie and Cockney. What happened next was akin to a tennis match. We said something, Geordies looked at Bob, he translates, they laugh, they say something, we look at Bob, he translates, we laugh. This carried on all night and Bob commented on how well I was holding up under the relentless "E" onslaught and how I'd not made an "Exhibition" of myself yet. No pun intended, obviously. Words spoken too soon, I'm afraid.

Now, if you're a drinker, you'll know that booze and fresh air don't mix too well and so it was with me. We walked back to their house, I sat down and answered every question with a monosyllabic grunt. It was then that they all realised I'd taken a turn for the worse. I got up and headed for the sink. No worries. I threw up all over dishes that were piled up waiting to be washed, and then realising what I'd done, compounded the felony by sifting through the sick with my hands and chucking the big bits in the bin. I bet Bob's wife loves Londoners. We, the first ones in her house, return her hospitality by

Steve throwing up a.m. and me throwing up p.m. Much more spectacularly, though, if I do say so myself.

Micky and Steve got a cab and took me back to the guest house. Micky slept on the floor of Steve's room. We got up the next morning and this time three of us had "The Full English". The waiter looked at us quizzically. He knew something had changed, but couldn't put his finger on what. We left after breakfast and had a wander around town on a quiet Sunday morning. We bought a local paper and some bottled Newcastle Brown and Amber, which we were taking back as holiday gifts for some mates down in London. I felt amazingly well considering my Oliver Reed style exploits of the previous couple of days. We had a bit of time to spare, so we went into a café at the bus station. It was here that we had what can best be described as the "Heart Attack Special", a bap oozing with grease and so much artery clogging fat that you could almost feel it bunging up you heart valves with every mouthful. Still, with Homer Simpson determination and flying in the face of common sense, we finished it off. We got our bus and finished our weekend off by having a Whist drive on the way home. Just the usual weekend, then?

CHAPTER 12

BRIGADOON MYSTERY TOURS

THERE SEEMS TO be a general consensus amongst coach drivers that as long as they find the town we are playing in, then they're job's done. "Okay, we're here, let's play spot the ground." I've been on quite a few away trips, usually "up north" and on a midweek night, when this policy was admirably carried out.

The title of this chapter relates to my first two trips to Burnley. These were in fact both on Saturday afternoon, but the principal still applied. Burnley doesn't appear to be on any motorway signs or so it seems. The only time you realise you're in Burnley is when it magically appears. Countryside, countryside, wallop! Burnley. It always gives me the impression that this is Lancashire's "Brigadoon", although this one appears a bit more frequently, i.e. when home games are on. I get the impression that if you look back towards the town once you'd left, it would have disappeared. It may be the drugs, but it would explain why it's not sign-posted, wouldn't it?

My first trip up there to a pre-renovated ground on April Fools Day, 1995, was by club coach. We'd arrived at the ground less than mob handed for a meaningless (for us anyway) end of season Division One game which we won 2-1. It wasn't so much the game as the journey that was interesting. We took a weird route. We hit Huddersfield at about 1.00pm and went straight through town on to a road running up the side of Saddleworth Moor. Fuck me! What a place. It looks like an inhospitable alien planet. What those evil bastards did to those kids here came into focus when you see up close just how bleak and hostile they're execution place was.

We carried on through what looked like the set of *Emmerdale*, Hebdon Bridge, flint walls, fields, sheep, it's all a bit much for a city dweller like me. Halifax, that's better. Civilisation if that's the word for it. Marvellous countryside, very cloth cap and whippet, hills, rivers, etc., Burnley.

My next trip took an entirely different route through Blackburn's red bricked, cobbled street and mosque minareted landscape. As we arrived here at 2.30pm or so, we thought he'd got confused and was heading for Ewood Park instead. No, we came out the other side and found the mystic citadel that is Turf Moor, now a bit more posh than before. We arrived just as it kicked off. I hate this as it throws me out of kilter. Ideally I need to go into a self-induced higher state to be able to watch Millwall. I saw this one raw, and as it was under Jimmy Nicholl, I can assure you that sedation was preferable. I think we lost, but during this era of management, I tried to blank it all out. Sorry.

Twice I've been to matches midweek up north, when we've actually got lost and stopped to pick up a local to take us to the ground. Quite what stopped these individuals taking the coach to their destination, buggering off and leaving you none the wiser, I don't know. It's all a bit chancy, I'd have thought. I'm no driver, but wouldn't a map be better?

The first time it happened was for a night match at Tranmere in 1991 on a freezing cold Bonfire Night. We drove past the chemical plant or whatever it is that looks like a cross between Moon Base Alpha and *Bladerunner*, we got lost and picked up a local Scouser (?) who very kindly directed us to our customary defeat. 2-1 I think in this instance. The game was played against a backdrop of "Whizz bang Ooh! Aah!", etc. and surprisingly we had a bloody awful ref. No really we did. Prenton Park was pre-renovation as well, although our "open to the elements" terrace did give us a better view of the fireworks, I suppose, so that's something.

My other "local" guided mystery tour was at Oldham again in midweek in 1995. We hit the outskirts of the town and stopped, lost again. Where's a boy scout when you need one? We asked some "locals", they didn't know, so we had to send someone to the nearest mini cab office. They claimed not to know either. I think if we had all disembarked and ordered a dozen cabs, the Oldham A-Z might have come out of the draw a bit sharpish! It would have been the only time where the "You must have come in a taxi!" chant was apposite. Once again we picked up a local and he took us to the ground. We drew 2-2 with two very late Millwall goals.

Another good tactic adopted by the coach driver is to aim for the lights, a great idea on paper, but for a night match in Birmingham the problems are two-fold:

1) It's not exactly hospitable to us and

2) It's a bloody big place and a light on the skyline could be anything, so we then have to drive around until you either find a heavy police presence or you spot people walking towards something in an "I'm on my way to a game" manner.

The "lighthouse" theory was adopted for both of my night visits, firstly for a 0-0 game in 1993, which had a linesman who put his flag up as soon as a Millwall player as much as bent a blade of grass, in encroaching into Birmingham's half. Now I'm all for consistency, but I can't believe that Birmingham have a foolproof offside system. Perhaps the linesman, sorry, Assistant Referee (or arsehole's little helper as might be more apt), is just a useless pillock, who knows. And secondly for a Worthington Cup First Round 1st leg defeat in 1998.

This foolproof ground detection system was also used at Macclesfield for a midweek match in 1999, when taking the line from *Poltergeist* about "heading into the light" literally meant we were drawn moth-like to the brightness only to find that it was a garden centre.

I went to Wigan on a Friday night in April 1998 to visit the old tip that they used to play at prior to their ground move, which is a vast improvement. For this game we arrived at Wigan and then drove around and around. We appeared to keep passing the same places of interest, pubs mostly, and Wigan Pier. "Get your bucket and spade, Arkwright we're off down t'beach!" Good luck.

I think the "aim for the light" tactic was stymied because I doubt Springfield Park actually had any floodlights, the lighting being supplied by a mass raising of lighters a la a Scorpions concert. Whatever the reason, we did have a bit of a job finding it, drew 0-0 to preserve our divisional status, were met by enough security to stop the Kosovan conflict, and broke down outside the ground. We stood contemplating how to get home and what to do. Go into Wigan's club, go to the pub or stand and watch the dawn come up over Wigan? One of my life's ambitions as you can imagine, very romantic I'm sure and obviously I'd loved to have stayed, but sadly the coach home situation was remedied and off we went.

Another night match to Swansea on a Friday night in the FA Cup was driven almost all the way through South Wales in darkness. This added to the air of menace, as if it needed any assistance.

Finally, we took three coaches to Southampton in 1989, the season we got relegated from the old Division One. We won 2-1 in what was the opening game of the season. En route, our coach driver, in an effort to give us a thorough look at the countryside, got lost in a village with a road only wide enough for a car, not a small coach convoy. Somehow we managed to turn around, got to the ground at 2.55pm, and pulled up outside of the away end - only for the police to insist we park up half a mile away and walk back. Why? Search me! Which they did.

CHAPTER 13

HILLSBOROUGH – IT COULD HAVE BEEN US

ON SATURDAY THE 1st of April, 1989, in the old First Division, we played Sheffield Wednesday at Hillsborough. I travelled up to this match by train with Micky and Steve, we walked from Wadsley Bridge station towards the ground and as befits most Millwall away games, the pubs on the way were either shut or "bouncered".

We arrived at the gates, entered the ground and walked out onto a wide concourse. We'd decided to stand, so we walked towards the middle of the terracing. We went through a narrow tunnel, which quite honestly was a bit claustrophobic even when empty. The terrace was sparsely populated as the bulk of our support were sitting in the stand above us. We lost 3-0. This end was the Leppings Lane terrace. Now trust me, it isn't with the benefit of hindsight, I can assure you, but I remember thinking on the day how lax the stewarding seemed to be.

Two weeks later, disaster struck on this very same terrace. This for me was brought into sharper focus due to the proximity of my visit being so close to the tragedy. We played at West Ham, a highly volatile game for us at best on Saturday the 22nd of April, a week after this disaster. Prior to kick-off, a silence in respect of the dead was due to happen. In scenes that made me ashamed to be a Millwall supporter for the only time in my life, a few morons quite close to me made some derogatory comments during this "silence". These were shouted down by the bulk of the decent fans present. In truth it was only a few brainless pricks who made the comments, but, obviously from the "Chicken Run" to my right, it sounded like a mass insult to the dead. Not true, but I could understand their reaction. The temperature of the already highly charged game went up a notch and West Ham started hurling "Scum!" style abuse at us.

Millwall lost 3-0 and to be truthful, I couldn't have cared less after the "silence" debacle. I know I hadn't personally insulted anyone, but as a Millwall fan I'm tarred with the same brush as the people who did. It did make me despair for the mentality of these people, even if you don't like a particular club, Liverpool in this case. The people who died were ordinary fans just like us. These are the sort of arseholes who would probably have cheered if it had been one of our more intense rivals, West Ham for example, who'd died.

I can only assume that these people had not been at Hillsborough a couple of weeks prior as the "there but for the grace of God" aspect would have added a poignancy to the minute's silence, which would have shut them up.

A couple of things did occur to me, though, having visited the ground so close to the semi final game. Why were pubs that were off limits to us opened for this game? I assume they must have been, as it's been reported, truthfully or not, that the late arrival of fans who had been drinking was to blame. I therefore assume that this drinking was done in local pubs. I apologise if my assumption is incorrect. Also, in true "disaster waiting to happen" fashion, they put the club with fewer fans into the biggest end and vice versa.

The reason I mention Hillsborough, apart from the fact that I was there two weeks prior, is that on other occasions it could have been us. I've been at several matches where for one reason or another over-crowding in the away section has occurred.

In 1978 we played Tottenham, Hoddle and all, at White Hart Lane in an old Division Two game, as Spurs had been relegated, and we were marshalled on to the Park Lane terrace. As is usual for these type of games we'd taken a very large following. Behind the goal we were packed in so tight that Colin and I were literally off our feet the whole game. Not a pleasant feeling. In truth the only respite we got was when we scored - three times as it happened – and the "sardines" all jumped about and for a few moments created some room. It was the same for the game in Division One in 1988 when again we were off our feet. Prior to the kick-off I had to lift a terrified boy to safety who was too scared to stand in the jam packed terrace. I managed to get him to the relative safety of the gangway and to a steward. Now you will say this isn't as bad as Hillsborough. True, but it would only have needed a late surge to put us all in serious danger.

Something that nearly happened on the terrace at QPR for a League Cup game in the 80s when a last minute influx meant I was crushed against a barrier for the whole game and outside West Brom for the 5-1 defeat in 1983, when the masses trying to get in were crushed against a wall, because in their infinite wisdom only a couple of turnstiles were opened to let the thousands of us in.

We played at Arsenal in 1988 in an FA Cup Third Round game, which we lost 2-0. The press prior to this match had circulated the absurd story about how we were going to steal the clock at the Clock

End. You'd have a job getting a Swiss Army knife into the ground, let alone a crane. Still, never let the real world interfere with any drink induced fantasies. For this match we all naturally assumed that the game would be all ticket and that we'd be given the whole of one end, our thinking being as follows:

1) We'd not played Arsenal in most people's lifetimes, so a huge following would go.

2) This end could be isolated and kept more secure should any clashes occur.

3) As I mentioned, if it was all-ticket you could control numbers and segregation easier.

Instead it was first come first served and we were given only half the Clock End and a bit of the West Stand. Colin, Steve Kimberley and I went to this game. We arrived early – about 1.00pm – as we knew from experience what it would be like. Sure enough as time progressed it was absolutely packed. Once again we found ourselves crushed together and off our feet. A late arrival of fans to the left clashed with police in an effort to get in. I assume the Police had sanctioned the ticket allocation, or lack of it, and segregation policy for the day. These clashes were caused by over-crowding when people justifiably trying to get into the ground were man-handled by the police.

Needless to say the clock remained intact. It wouldn't fit on my wall anyway, but again this situation could have got totally out of control and in my humble opinion a more sensible policy as highlighted earlier would probably have nipped any problems in the bud. Naturally these incidents were used in the press to spread fear about the likely outcome of Millwall's imminent promotion to Division One, i.e. "The Vikings are coming!"

The much publicised and hyped Luton FA Cup Quarter Final at Kenilworth Road was in truth the game when people could very easily have died and I don't mean from flying seats! I drove up to Luton with Steve K, we got there for some reason at about 4.30pm, I had the flu and had actually been coughing up blood earlier, so I was in perfect fettle for this game. Several things became apparent, even at this early stage. There was little or no police presence and there seemed to be an air of anarchy.

Luton adopted a policy I can only imagine was financial and decided not to make this game all ticket, I presume on the assumption that Millwall were a Division Three side and not attracting big crowds at the time and thus would not bring masses to Luton. However, this was a massive Cup game for us and any lapsed Millwall fan was bound to go the short trip up the M1. We knew this, why didn't Luton and the police?

It has been said that Watford, our other possible opponents, had actually already printed tickets for this game, on the assumption that they'd beat Luton. True or not, this most certainly should have happened here.

When Steve and I arrived, people were roaming about everywhere. Several incidents had already occurred with some broken windows and run-ins with the predominantly Asian shop owners. When we got to the ground at about 5.30pm or so, it was said hundreds had already got in through a broken turnstile and when normality returned, we went in ourselves.

The away end at the time was an open terrace at the opposite end to where it is now. I would guess that it held about 5,000-6,000. It was divided into three sections, separated into three pens by box girder type fences. We also had an anti-invasion fence surrounding the pitch in front of us. This penning in wasn't too comfortable, particularly as I'm slightly claustrophobic and was also ill to boot.

As the match approached, the pens were getting overfilled and people were sitting all along the dividing girders, thus making it difficult to view anything other than what was directly in front of you. From my position in the middle block, I could see that the section to my right was getting dangerously overcrowded, so much so that people were lifting kids, etc, over the top of the fence and on to the pitch. This prompted more people to scale the fence and go into the empty side seating. These events were described as pitch invasions in much the same way that Hillsborough had been.

A friend of mine, Lee, who'd gone to the game, was in this section and said it was terrifying. He's 6ft and a rugby playing brown belt in karate, so what on earth was it like for smaller, less able bodied people? He's also an Arsenal supporter, who went along with some work and rugby mates. This sort of thing also happens at Millwall – see "Wembley". Naturally all the extenuating circumstances were totally ignored in favour of the "riot" footage. I know some will say I'm an apologist for Millwall, but I admit totally that the trouble at Luton did indeed happen, but in typical fashion if someone had actually died in the crush in this pen, perhaps it might have been seen in its real light, i.e. an ill-conceived "disaster waiting to happen".

I honestly don't think that the 1-0 defeat had much of a bearing on the ensuing "Melee on the telly". I do know, however, that if you are intent on trouble, then a lack of police, and for the police who are there to turn tail and run, probably isn't the best strategy.

To my mind this was a cock-up of biblical proportions. Unticketed, badly organised and woefully under-policed. If I were the organisers, or disorganisers in their case, I would feel very, very fortunate that I didn't have people's lives on my hands. I was actually there and whilst the riot and other misdemeanours did occur and were perpetrated by Millwall, the whole story, in its entirety is more sinister in my view, where people could have been crushed to death by trying to fit a very large quart into a pint pot, purely for financial gain.

CHAPTER 14

LOVELY DAY FOR IT

BEING ENGLAND, THE weather's taken its toll over the years. I've been on enough open terraces to top up my ruddy old sea dog complexion and save for volcanoes and plagues of frogs, I've had the lot. The weather usually saves its excesses for open to the elements terraces or it waits until you're in the street outside, so that you get the full value for your money.

WIND: Not mine, the climate's. I always think that wind, radish induced or God's work, is the worst weather to play in. It surprises me that save for structural problems with the stands, games are rarely called off. Still I'm not Graham Kelly, thank God, or whichever old duffer is in charge these days, so I don't make the rules. Consequently I've been to many "breezy" games, but two recent games were played in the equivalent of "Hurricane Betsy". You'll think this is sour grapes because we lost both games, but of course it's not, perish the thought.

We played at Hartlepool for our now traditional FA Cup First Round "minnows" defeat, only 1-0 in this case. Now I don't know if it's always like that there, but the home kit is a sou'wester, so that might be a clue. This game consisted of airborne punts floating in the air, goal kicks coming straight back to you, and corner flags blown flat. We also played at Chesterfield and lost 2-0. Low flying Chesterfield, as they say, at the time. Just as well as I wouldn't want to be a kite in these conditions.

The wind is what they call a great leveller or unwatchable farce, if you prefer. At Chesterfield we also had driving rain for good measure. This prompted us to put our programmes back on the coach before the game to protect them. I suppose it would have made more sense to leave the programme inside the ground and sit on the coach ourselves. I didn't think of that!

HAIL: Not Caesar, but the bloody weather. At Brighton in the early Nineties for a glorious 0-0 game, we were treated to nature in all its splendour, when we got battered with hail all afternoon on a thankfully uncovered side terrace. Who wants a roof? I'd have missed every face stinging, eye watering hailstone otherwise.

We sat high up in the away stand at Stoke's Britannia Stadium. This gave us the perfect opportunity to get a good view of the imminent approach of a hailstorm coming our way. I thought it was a bit strange when the hill behind the home stand suddenly disappeared, but I've watched enough X-Files to know this sort of thing happens all the time. Imagine my surprise, not to say relief, that it was only a hailstorm, albeit a humdinger, and not an ancient curse venting its rage upon us. This storm led to the pitch side turning white and for the game to be played out to a God inspired rhythmic roof thumping that Keith Moon would have been proud of.

COLD: As in brass monkeys. The coldest I've ever been was at Sheffield Wednesday for a midweek FA Cup replay, which we lost 2-0, after an incredible 4-4 first game, which also saw each side denied a goal. At this game I sat high up above the Leppings Lane terrace, my feet quite literally frozen to the spot. I had to hop about to try to get circulation going before I could walk back to the station. Now here's a thought for the Club Shop – what about producing a range of club badged moon boots for this eventuality? I'm sure they'd be very popular with the more fashion conscious amongst our fans. How about it?

As I've mentioned before, in the North East it's not uncommon to see people in club shirts in arctic conditions. I've not been up to Carlisle, so they might not wear shirts at all. They might just stand there bare backed and erect of nipple for all I know. If this progression is carried through in Scotland, they may well be stark bollock naked, save for a well placed sporran to cover their testimonials and to keep their programme in. I might be wrong, but best not to dwell on it.

It was in Newcastle on Christmas week on a Sunday in 1992 that it was a bit chilly even for these hardy souls. Cold enough for Captain Oates to think twice about leaving the tent in the first place, I'd say. The pitch was half frozen with frost. I think the only reason it was played was because it was a live ITV Sunday match. I'd not thought about sitting in the warm watching it when I could get frostbite being there. Where's the fun in that?

It was minus four and despite 14 layers of clothing and insulating my body with goose fat, it was still a tad nippy, particularly as we waited for our "Black Maria" adventure back to the station after the game.

I've been to Barnsley five times in all to date and whether it's the height of summer or the depths of winter, it's been bloody cold, particularly on the nice open terrace conveniently exposed to the elements blowing off the dales, moors, ridings? Whatever, what do I know, I'm a soft Southerner, but I'd certainly not go on Ilkley Moor without my hat, woolly muffler, gloves, or a mug of hot soup, I can tell you.

It's not only up north. At Bristol Rovers on Boxing Day, 1999, I can honestly say that we got drenched, frozen and sleeted on. Nothing like a bit of variety. We didn't thaw out until we got back to London, with the heater on all the way back in the car. We did seriously contemplate watching the game from inside the toilet at the back of the terrace, if we could have made a big enough viewing hole. As I said, I may just be a southern Jessie and everyone north of Watford might consider these conditions quite balmy.

RAIN: Unfortunately not in Spain, but on my bloody head! The daftest rain affected match I've been at was actually at The Old Den v Wolves in the early 90s. Again it was a live ITV match. On the way to the ground the heavens opened and we got soaked. Thanks, I'd have hated to have been under cover and missed it. Now this can have been the only way the ref (in snorkel and flippers) can have seen the conditions as fit for anything other than water polo. You get the idea. Win the toss to decide who's in the shallow end first. We won 2-0 in the equivalent of a kick about in a paddling pool.

For the "infamous" Ian Wright coin throwing game at Highbury, a 1-1 draw, we were fine until we started our walk back to the station, wherever that was. We wandered around only vaguely aware of our final destination in the mother of all monsoons. We actually got a bus in the end, which drove us through feet of water in some streets on the way home. Unfortunately I'm not exaggerating. My coat shrank and my programme turned into papier mache, Micky's coat only fitted his small son afterwards. Were we down-hearted? Bloody right we were.

The most perverse water incident was at Port Vale on New Year's Day, 1991. The walk from the station is about 25 miles, or so it seems, past the jolly local hostelries. I got to the ground and bought a programme. Prophetically the front cover showed an action shot of Charlton's recent visit, with the background sky looking like Armageddon and Charlton foolishly without anoraks. This cover was an omen if I've ever seen one. Mystic Meg printers? Probably not, because knowing her accuracy it would have been a heatwave.

Anyway we won 2-0 amidst a continual downpour. After the game we walked back to the station and got a "drowned rat" makeover. The journey home on the train, in a treat for any closet pervs in our midst, saw most people take their clothes off to try and dry them out. A very bizarre sight it was too, like something out of a Derek Jarman film. Not that I've ever seen one, obviously. Never mind gay, I'm not even cheerful.

Another marketing idea, this time for British Rail or whatever they're called this week. Why don't they open a franchise of on board "wishy washy" launderettes for this eventuality. Just a thought.

Once at Bristol City on another "damp" afternoon, Simon and I drove up on a club coach, Simon in an "I'm alright Jack" waterproof coat. The driver of the coach actually parked inside the ground and we sat on it until kick-off, steamed up windows obscuring our view. Very Tina Turner, but not for the same reason obviously.

At Reading in 1999/2000 we had sun and rain and a double rainbow. We found out after the game that the only omen this portrayed was two goals for the home side. Spooky.

SNOW: Snow, quick, quick snow. We lost at home to Charlton in the snow for the first time in 250 years, so I don't like snow.

END OF THE WORLD: "We're all doomed I tell you!" The most surreal trip away I can recall was to Oldham in 1991. We were up challenging at the top of the table and in my first visit there, we got off the special train and asked a local plod where the ground was. He said "It's about five minutes walk".

Now based on the man's timekeeping skills, I wouldn't let him boil an egg for your breakfast if I were you. We set off across roads, motorways, roundabouts, grass verges . . . and 25 short minutes later we arrived at Boundary Park, again an open terrace. Oh joy! Picture the scene:

1) It's pissing down.

2) The colour of the sky is like a two day old bruise, i.e. yellow and purple.

3) The pitch is plastic and consequently an odd grey/green colour anyway.

4) The floodlights are on from the off, if that makes sense, which only added to the general weirdness of it all.

We drew 1-1, got soaked and wended home on our adventure back to the station.

Come to think of it, maybe watching football on TV is better. Nah!

CHAPTER 15

GET OFF MY SISTER!

LONDON: A BIT of background information for you tourists out there on our beloved capital: The streets are paved with gold, filled with Pearly Kings and Queens (of both sexes). We all eat only jellied eels, boiled beef and carrots, and pie and mash. We all have sing songs in the boozer standing around the old Joanna and are partial to the odd knees up! Very odd in some cases. In the East End, everyone can leave their doors open and be in and out of each other's houses, no worries, honest. This can prompt the odd unscheduled house clearance though. We all talk like Dick Van Dyke in *Mary Poppins* and are all as chirpy as a sparrow and no mistake, Governor!

In the West End a different tribe exists, who eat tofu and drink cappucinos in open air street front bistros and all at a King's ransom price. Beware. For North and South London, see East End.

Local visits are usually as eventful as trips outside "The Smoke", but it does mean you get home earlier. Before I start, I've got a confession to make. I've never been to Barnet. Naturally I'm filled with remorse at this, I'm terribly sorry. I thought I'd "take you by the hand and lead you round the grounds of London," so here goes in no particular order.

FULHAM: "This very picturesque piece of prime position real estate". Sorry! Old dump of a ground. Has some good and some odd memories. In recent years we've won 2-1 with nine men and got a 4-1 hammering on Fulham's promotion night. Mostly these games have been as memorable for the chants as for the games, with much Peschisolido/wife abuse as previously listed, England's finest Kevin Keegan and slightly balding Ray Wilkins also getting some stick, but mostly for Al Fayed who's had to withstand "Where's your Dodi gone?" and "We've got a passport, you ain't't/You'll never get a passport" chants. Why he didn't feel Millwall at home was a suitable game to show Michael "King of Pop" Jackson around, as he did for an earlier game, I don't know. Do you know children? Oops! Probably not a good choice!

We witnessed a rather limp promotion celebration and I'd say that in recent years the "Cottage" is a bit quaint and the away terracing borders on the dangerous, with a scandalous lack of facilities. Still you don't get a "shit load of cash" by spending any do you?

In the past I've watched games in the park behind with many others, during boring games in the 70s, only to be met by bemused looks when shouting for a penalty or cheering a goal that had nothing to do with the main game in front of everyone else. I've seen the boat race, or at least a boat race, go past years ago and I've heard a man with a nose like Steve Martin in *Roxanne* say to Alan Mullery of Fulham "Mullery, you've got a big nose!" without a hint of irony.

I've seen home fans thrown in the Thames and been stuck in a tunnel on an underground train home, behind a Millwall wrecked train with steamy windows. There goes Tina Turner again! We were all crammed together with cries of "Leave my arse alone!" emanating from my mate at the time, Paul White, who thought it hilarious.

LEYTON ORIENT: Family club alert! "Orient (clap, clap, clap)!" Terrifying, it is. This is a place I've been to numerous times, seen wins, defeats, draws, and more "drawers" hung on the line in the gardens behind the old away end. To be honest usually it's more interesting in the street than inside the ground. Leyton High Road usually adopts the policy I've highlighted earlier of shut down. I have seen Millwall rampage up and down this road in years gone by, so it was probably quite a good idea. One such game ended with police horses on Leyton station.

I once saw somebody have an epileptic fit on the Main Road. Nothing to do with football, but very disturbing to witness.

As I've been to the O's so many times, all the games merge into one. One I do recall, for obvious reasons, is a 5-3 defeat in 1984. Also, in the middle 70s I did go to Orient dressed in my "skinhead" apparel, complete with club scarves. I walked down on to Mile End station on to an empty eastbound central line platform, looked across to the westbound platform only to see hundreds of West Ham supporters en route to Arsenal. Oops! Luckily they either didn't see me or thought I must be a trap. You know, sort of "surely Millwall wouldn't come here single handed, no! It must be a trap!" The wait for the train dragged on a bit, in my mind anyway. Suffice to say I was very glad when it did arrive.

I walked to the ground to meet up with my mates in the West Stand which we just commandeered each visit, no arguments. On the way I went through a park outside the ground. Two old dears were sitting on a park bench. On seeing me one of them said something like "There you are, Ethel. That's one of them yobbos!" First impressions, eh? I could have been a stamp collecting, philosophy major for all they knew. Of course I wasn't, I was a "skinhead" type dressed in the uniform, with Millwall scarves, so they were probably right.

After this particular game hundreds of us boarded a train back to Mile End to confront West Ham coming back from Highbury. We got off the train and immediately started chanting "Bring on the West Ham" to a tune popular on Branston Pickles TV ads at the time – "Bring out the Branston". No sign of West Ham, so on to Whitechapel to try there. We found some, and much shouting and running about ensued. You know the type of thing.

WEST HAM UNITED: In my mind the people immediately north and south of the river are inherently the same. Let's be honest, there's only a few hundred feet of water or so between us, but for some reason Millwall are much more volatile. Don't ask me why. This close proximity to each other has developed into open hostility in the last 20 or 30 years, with a couple of deaths, incidents during Harry Cripp's testimonial at The Den, clashes outside The Den, a TV police programme about West Ham's trip to confront Millwall and the bi-weekly clashes at Whitechapel and Shadwell stations that used to be the norm a few years ago.

I often wonder why West Ham don't get the same media response for their fan's antics that we do. They've had pitch invasions to campaign against their Bond scheme, they're sponsored by Doctor Martens, and had their own hooligan documentary in the 70s, the equivalent of our *Panorama* hatchet job. Any one of the above would have led to an avalanche of "Roll of shame, fine them, shut them down" style reporting that we usually get. I can only assume the '66 World Cup and the "academy of football" image must offset the negative aspects.

In the 70s and 80s, Bobby Moore had a couple of pubs in the East End, one of which was in Stratford called Mooro's. He also had a sports shop opposite West Ham's ground, and for some reason I got strange looks when I tried to buy some Millwall stuff in there. Can't think why. A friend of mine, Ian and I, decided to go to Mooro's some time in the 80s for a few sherbets. Now stood at the bar while most of the inhabitants sang "I'm forever blowing bubbles!" and the like. I felt right at home, naturally. For some reason I didn't think bursting into "No one likes us!" or "Let 'em come!" was the best choice I could have made, so I stayed mute.

At closing time the bar staff said, "Can we have your glasses please?" Most of the people in the pub obliged by throwing them back at the bar, so me and Ian stood there ducking a barrage of Ravenhead, the ideal end to a good night out. A truly "Black Bart's Saloon" theme pub, run by the Chinners brewery it was too. Marvellous.

One notable game was in the Simod Cup in the 80s, which I didn't go to, I knew what it was going to be like and I couldn't be arsed for a nothing game. Lo and behold an 11,000 crowd, 20,000 police and a sky filled with a flotilla of helicopter gunships, we won as well, so serves me right.

On my visits to Upton Park in recent years, usually for games at 6.00am on Thursday morning to avoid trouble, I've been thoroughly searched, passed through metal detectors, and on a couple of occasions, stuck in a corner pen of the South Bank for what can best be described as a poxy "view" (sic).

When West Ham came to The Den for a game in 1990, the match as I mentioned was shown on a *Crimewatch* style transport police programme showing the happy Hammers mob's journey across London. For this game I'd arranged to meet Micky and Steve at Whitechapel on the East London line platform as usual. The pubs around the station were full of Millwall singing. I got down on to the platform and into a mass of West Ham. The sounds of conflict upstairs filled the air and this prompted the police to shut all the entrance barriers to the platform and order everyone on the train – I was on my own as my mates had not yet arrived.

West Ham were quite "up" on the train. I had a couple of small Millwall badges on, no colours. I got a few threatening looks on the train, but was quite amused at how quiet my travelling companions had now become upon arrival at New Cross Gate. "Rabbit, rabbit, rabbit – stum!" There was no Police to speak of and no segregation. Well done! I'd obviously not meant to reach the ground so early, but at 1.30pm I was on the Cold Blow Lane terrace, West Ham dispersed to God knows where.

Just before kick-off Micky and Steve came to join me at our usual spot and told of the battles outside. Bricks, bottles, running about, you know the sort of thing. Or perhaps you don't. I'm sure the police were thinking, "How did that happen?" Well I wonder.

ARSENAL: I've mentioned the FA Cup game at Highbury already, but we seem to play them on a regular basis in the Cups lately, culminating in our glorious 2-0 win at Highbury a few years ago, which I missed due to an Australian holiday. A few games do stick out in my mind. In the season that the Gunners won the league at Anfield, we played them at Highbury, thrashed them 0-0 in a massively one sided game, which had a brilliant Les Briley goal disallowed for offside when Teddy Sheringham was deemed to be interfering with play when standing next to the corner flag for a shot some 25 yards out. Top decision, lino!

We missed a hatful of chances, in a season when, for some of it we were challenging for the title ourselves and even topped the table ("Give me a slap, I think I'm dreaming!"). At this game we were packed into a corner of the Clock End. Some young blokes standing near us were smoking dope and somehow managed to drop their gear on the floor. As you couldn't get a fag paper between us, the chances of recovering their stash was nil. Thank the Lord it's not addictive, or we'd have had a mass cold turkey on our hands.

We again drew, this time 1-1, in a League Cup first leg game, with the surreal North Bank "singing mural". We stood along the West Side of the ground, we took the lead, Ian Wright kicked Millwall's Colin Cooper about six feet up in the air, and got roundly abused - "You black cunt!" and the like. He wasn't getting this abuse prior to the tackle, but within minutes he'd hit the deck with shrapnel wounds from a 50p piece that magically emerged from the crowd, hit his head, and then mysteriously vanished. Perhaps he should have an X-ray as it might have burrowed into his skull on impact. Cue . . . "Hit the deck, clutch face, roll about" = equity card = own chat show. You can follow the career path, can't you?

For the record I was hit with coins at Man City. They just bounced off. As I mentioned, I'd done karate for several years and been hit very powerfully by black belts and not felt the urge to writhe in agony. You've got to ask just how mighty was this coin? It did give *The Sun* the customary witch hunt opportunity. "Find the thug in the bobble hat!" Easy, go find the fashion police, they've already got him.

After the home FA Cup tie in 1995, battle raged at The Blind Beggar in Whitechapel. Everyone knew this was going to happen, so as I sat indoors in Stepney having my dinner, I heard police sirens screaming and thought "Ah! Kicking off time". This was highlighted in our local paper, *The East London Advertiser*, replete with club badges. High recognition indeed in my book.

QPR: A bit pokey, isn't it? Like being in an oversized match box. Just be thankful I'm not claustrophobic. What? I am? Oh, shit!

I've sat in the away stand at Loftus Road, next to Danny Baker's Dad. How's that for name dropping? Unless you strategically position yourself, you can't see the goal at your own end. Still, as Millwall don't usually bother to attack here, it makes no odds.

We did win once on a Southend beach of a pitch in the old Division One, when the goals were very conveniently scored up at the other end. I came back from holiday in Australia in the year we beat Arsenal and Chelsea in the FA Cup, to put a personal end to the run by turning up at Loftus Road and using my "Jonah" like powers to make Damian Webber "Ask for permission to go to the toilet" the very instant that a QPR cross came over in the last minute. Penalty, 1-0, there you are, mission accomplished. Sorry!

For a League Cup game at Loftus Road in 1993, myself, Simon and Mad Ted sat high in the home stand and strained our necks to see the goal beneath us. We lost, our fans pelted QPR defender Alan McDonald with coins, Mad Ted got attacked by a woman in front of him for using foul language and for dropping his chewing gum down her coat. So nothing unusual there then. We headed home via White City underground, stood on the train with the doors shut and exchanged pleasantries with the locals who showed a bravado not usually associated with their team. For some reason when the tube doors opened, their steely defiance evaporated to jelly fish proportions. How strange.

The only time out of my numerous visits when I've stood up was for a League Cup game in 1987. The first leg at QPR saw Millwall, an old Division Two side, against QPR, a First Division side. The game was played out to a hell of a racket by us, accompanied by much rhythmic seat banging. This prompted QPR's then manager, Jim Smith, to call it "The night of the zulus". We narrowly lost 2-1 and thought we'd win at home. Based on what it was like in the first leg, Bald Eagle decided that he would have to negate The Old Den crowd's influence. He instigated a crowd muting tactic that consisted of Terry Fenwick passing to David Seaman pre back pass rule. He rolls back to Fenwick and this continues for 90 minutes. We drew 0-0. Still, it did lull the crowd, most of whom were in a tedium induced coma by half-time.

At the first leg at QPR I got in the ground early and took up a position near the back. Fine until a late surge left me crushed against a barrier and underneath some piping, which at half time ominously dripped "fluid" all over us. Now I'm not going to mention the likely source of the pipe's contents, but I think eau de toilet(te), not eau de cologne, is more likely. I did get a seat on the train on the way home quite easily though for some reason.

CHELSEA: Away, always a treat. We played them twice in one season in 1984/5. I went to both away games with Steve K. The day's radio reports were talking of outbreaks of unpleasantness all over the place, so we decided a "Watch your backs" policy was advisable. For the first game in the League Cup first leg we lost 3-1, got to the ground just after kick-off and watched the game from a great distance. I used to hate going to the "old" Stamford Bridge as you needed binoculars. Still, we did get a goal so we might have a chance. The return a 1-1 draw at The Den was the most hostile atmosphere I can recall, even for a night match, as I've mentioned.

Later in the same season we played them again, away, in an FA Cup Fourth Round game. Steve K had a bad back and propped himself up against a barrier. Unfortunately for him, we won 3-2, prompting much jumping about and back slapping. Speedie missed a penalty at our end and we had a massive clock behind us which in true style took an hour to record each minute. I recall 82 minutes being on the board forever, but still we won, did I mention that? At both of these games and for a Division One game in 1989, Millwall fans set light to advertising hoardings at the back of the away terrace. Still, once you've established a tradition, it's a shame to stop it, don't you think?

Chelsea sang "Is that all you take away?" to our packed end to which we cheerfully replied "It's enough to do you cunts!" You can't beat a bit of witty banter, can you? We played a Saturday game in the old First Division, my first daylight visit with Millwall. We had numerous chances and somehow lost 4-0. We continued the great arsonist tradition, it would be rude not to, and several thousand of us gathered in the road outside. The police tried to contain us outside the ground, but were losing control and the police horses trying to control the surges were getting pushed over.

The idea was to funnel everyone on to Fulham Broadway station. If you've been on this tiny platform, you can imagine the outcome of thousands of people arriving at once. Not for me, I thought. I said to Micky and Steve "You go down there if you want, I'm going to walk to another station", which I did. They later told me of ticket collection boxes being pushed over, being crushed and surging on to over-crowded trains that would give the old Japanese shunter trains a run for their money. Sod that I'd thought, and I was right.

CRYSTAL PALACE: No one at Millwall seems to like Crystal Palace, for a myriad of different reasons. Nothing in particular, just a fact I'm afraid. Thought I'd mention it.

It's a place where we usually smash up Norwood Junction station, take over large chunks of the ground, suffer some bizarre ticketing policies, and to rouse the home fans from their stupor, we usually have to endure pre-recorded, crowd encouraging *Glad All Over* type tapes. Well I certainly find it inspiring anyway.

I've also seen Charlton and Wimbledon at Selhurst. Some people will get into bed with anybody. Again I've seen many, many games here, but one I do recall was at a top of the table Division One game in 1994, which we lost 1-0 thanks to Clive "score for everyone except us" Allen skying a sitter. Former Lion Chris Armstrong naturally scored against us. Ain't that always the way? Whilst this game wasn't a patch on a 4-3 defeat a few years prior, outside it was more interesting.

Two morons in full Palace garb greeted us with "Champions!" chants. Presumably they liked pain as that's what they got. Kicked, abused, punched and spat on. It was at this game that Mad Ted chased up the road, booting a considerably larger Palace fan up the arse. Strange but true.

BRENTFORD: This ground is famous for having four pubs, one on each corner. As Stan Bowles used to play for them, it was just as well it wasn't four bookies, otherwise they'd have needed to drag him kicking and screaming away from the 3.00pm at Newmarket in order to start the match.

Terry Hurlock used to play for Brentford pre Lions and was always roundly "gypoed" for his trouble.

I've been to this ground numerous times and a bit like Orient and Charlton, it's all a bit of a blur. Not a team that stirs the blood for us, I'm afraid. Before my time we did lob a hand grenade on to the pitch, a bit much even for us. This could have been a forerunner of pre Taylor report ground renovations, albeit unintended.

In the 1999 / 2000 season 3-1 victory leading to our play-off games, we had a run in with one particular ill advised Brentford supporter. Now I'm not sylph-like myself, but even I'm in a position to say that a massively stupid fat home fan dressed in a white coat made me look Kate Moss in comparison. He stood at the front of the home section berating us. He also threatened a Millwall fan sitting in the home stand and was the target of concerted abuse, lovingly gaining the nickname "fat cunt". He was lambasted with "FC, FC what's the score?" as we took charge, and then "FC, FC la la la la la!", "Is your Mum as fat as you?", "FC's, FC's Mum's a whore!", "FC is a virgin!", and after 20 minutes or so of this, "FC, FC's going to cry!"

This misguided fool left the verbal abuse frontline. We weren't sure if he'd gone for good or was just getting in an early shipping order for his half-time pie "gluttonfest". Sensibly he didn't return, so we'll never know.

In our previous visit it was also the site of Matthew Harding chants post fatal accident and the only game home or away that Billy Bonds got really abused, after a 2-1 defeat. He was an honest decent bloke, it appeared. Unfortunately he had a very dodgy lineage, as far as we were concerned anyway.

A similar thing happened for our game in September, 2000, when the management pairing of Millwall old boys, Stevens and McLeary, were barracked at the end of a dismal 1-1 draw. A game marred by the throwing of various missiles, resulting in a Brentford fan getting a nasty head wound while she sat in the home stand. Good old Ron Noades threatened to ban us in the future because of it. If this game was a sample of any in the future, he'll be doing us a favour.

It was a game also notable for the police surrounding the home fans and pushing them further back into the stand, prompting them to sing, "We're supposed to be at home!"

They also chanted that we only chucked coins at women. Not true. We threw a bottle as well, and as I've already mentioned, we've thrown a grenade in the past too, so there. As usual, the home fans "gave it large" in the ground, but were notable by their total absence outside the ground. Why bother?

TOTTENHAM: We drew 3-3 in 1978, lost 2-0 to a Gascoigne inspired Spurs in 1988, and lost 3-1 on Boxing Day the following season, both in the old Division One. For the second of these visits, Steve, Micky and I went. We were 3-0 down at half-time and Steve said, "That's it, I'm off," and went home. We did score, from a corner in this game, by Judas Cascarino, a triumph in itself as we don't usually score this way. I've mentioned the other off pitch antics elsewhere, so onwards and southwards.

CHARLTON: The Old Valley, eh? What a size. I've seen Charlton at all their many lodgings so many times it's not funny. I've seen Millwall lose once in a striped moon, let alone a blue one. The Old Valley had one massive side. Even dear old Eddie The Eagle would have got vertigo at the top. The pre-completed Valley had portastands, portaloos and portakabins, nowt else. I dare say it's like the San Siro now, but it certainly wasn't then.

A few incidents over the years do stand out. For some strange reason it was common, at least amongst my cousin's friends, to go to Millwall one week and Charlton the next. I don't know if everyone did this in the 60s/70s or whether it was just that my cousin's wife's brothers supported Charlton.

My earliest memory at the old pre-wanderlust Valley, though not my first visit, was for a vital game in April, 1972, which we won 2-0 when we were battling for promotion to the old Division One. We went to this game resplendent in Rod Stewart type tartan hats and scarves – fashion victims or what? But we were only young and our good taste gene wasn't developed, so forgive us. We'd only bought these hats the Sunday before and this was Tuesday. This was when Millwall would take over The Valley.

We stood in the "home" covered end, someone shouted "Here's Charlton!" and we all just ran at them. Me and my mate Paul were right at the front and got collared by the police who grabbed us round the neck and stole our hats – "For my son," my one told me. Perhaps the fashion police do indeed exist. Can you get nicked for poor dress sense? Probably not, because at Charlton I'm sure anoraks constitute a more heinous crime than ours and the police would be spoilt for choice.

For one game against Charlton on a Sunday at Upton Park, I went on my own and decided to sit in the stand as opposed to taking up my usual position on the South Bank for the normal lousy view. As a consequence, I managed to get back to Upton Park tube before the main bulk of our fans. Whilst standing on the platform surrounded by "Happy Valleyers" one of their number standing next to me uttered these words: "I hope the train gets here before them cunts do!"

Too late old chap. And that's not a very nice way to talk about your South London cousins is it? Naughty anorak, wash your mouth out with soap.

At Upton Park they once played us *The Lion Sleeps Tonight*. Not against you lot, he doesn't.

Finally at the partially revamped Valley for a game in the 90s, a couple of things stood out for this particular game. We arrived at "Portalooville" to be met by totally disinterested stewards who at 2pm didn't bother to check any tickets, as is usual for Millwall at away games. Everyone ignores ticket numbers and sits anywhere. This is what we did, quite a few of us, all with seats scattered all over, sat together. At 2.55pm, the real occupant of my seat arrived and insisted on sitting in it. There was a seat in front empty. No go, as the steward had now found out I was in the wrong seat and he demanded that I sit in my correct seat. As the stand was now full, I said (expletives deleted) "Why had you not already checked the tickets, old man, it's quite possible that my seat will be occupied. I do hope that the incumbent isn't too put out when you request that they vacate", or words to that effect – add in a few "F's" and "C's" and get Quentin Tarrantino to direct the scene. I think you may then get a more truthful picture.

I pointed out to this gentleman that if I didn't have a seat on arrival, I'd take retribution out on his head. So we get to the correct seat and "stripe me", it's full. So he, in a coup de grâce moment says "Well sit anywhere, then." I was too apoplectic and purple with rage to respond adequately as he shot off up the stairs. You can see why a steward's demise at Leicester, as previously mentioned, was so pleasing for me.

In the warm up prior to this game, this touching moment happened. Kim Grant, who later became a Millwall player, was running about quite close to us, when a voice from the crowd said "My sister's called Kim".

Kim laughs.

"Yeah! She's a shit cunt too!"

Kim doesn't laugh.

This game was notable for Pat Van Den Hauwe's debut. Within seconds of the start he'd knocked a Charlton player flat out with an elbow, in the area in front of us, thus endearing himself to us straight away.

WIMBLEDON: Plough Lane. "Toilet". Enough said. Except that the only toilets they did have were Charltonesque portaloos. For my last ever visit there, Vinny "hard man" Jones bottled it against a real "hard man", Terry Hurlock. I vowed to never go there ever again. I didn't know I couldn't anyway at the time. The style of play and appalling sportsmanship or lack of it and the fact that Plough Lane made The Old Den look like Old Trafford just didn't have any appeal to me. Never any trouble, though one year a mob, Chelsea I think, ran up the hill, saw how many of us there were, stopped and thought better of it. We played in a League Cup game at Selhurst against Millwall "old" boys. We got thumped 5-1 and made up 99% of the crowd. Still it's a bit far to go isn't it? Closer than Dublin though, I'd imagine.

WATFORD: Home of the Brimson Brothers' *Tales Of Mystery And Imagination*. I've not read their books because the notion of Watford being anything but a "family" club – the words "hooligan" and "Watford" don't go together too well – seems absurd to me. You could stand in Watford Town Centre or the home stand for that matter and go unimpeded for a fortnight. Two punch-ups with Luton a season does not a reputation make.

Scene of my first out of town away match and somewhere I've been to more times than you can shake a stick at, it's a nice ground now, save for one stand. Good of them to lay on an exercise course for the away fans. Feel the burn as you yomp through and around the allotments.

Years ago I saw a pre blonde crop David James – different image, but still flapping wildly – and a clown even amongst referees in the shape of Gurnam Singh for a match on my birthday in 1992. I'd like to thank him personally for getting the day's festivities off to such a comic start. Cheers.

It was also at Watford a couple of seasons back when Paul and Nathan had their first close-up example of the phenomenon that is Mad Ted. Simon, Patrick and Dave sat lower down in the stand as Patrick said he couldn't see properly. I sat nearer the back with Paul and Nathan and the aforesaid Mad Ted. He'd not been to many away matches for a while due to financial constraints, so for this game they sat with him at an away match for the first time and saw him ranting at a home fan who was sitting some 75 yards away. He carried this on for most of the game whilst Paul and Nathan looked bemused, as did all our near neighbours, who asked if he was with us. Yes he is, and we're proud of it!

CHAPTER 16

FROM RED HEAT
TO JUNGLE BOOK

I'm a veteran of many club coaches, too bloody many. Most people usually travel away by car or train. That leaves a few foolish souls to travel on the official coaches. Usually one or two coaches plus a Junior Lions coach and some pub coaches for bigger games. Now that special trains are a thing of the past, at least they are for us, a large convoy will travel. About 20 coaches went to Man City, for example. I heard that up to 100 coaches went to Forest with Charlton. That's a traffic jam in it's own right. They were free, I believe, so there you are.

At some away games, usually the more volatile ones, the police pick up the away coaches on the motorway and guide them to the ground. Where's the fun in that? On several occasions we've been boarded by local motorcycle or meat wagon coppers and given a "welcome" speech, usually in a thick local dialect we either can't understand or find highly amusing, so the man's attempt at public speaking is usually met with contempt and piss taking, in much the same style as our singing all the way through tannoy announcements. Nobody is particularly interested and just wants to get to the ground.

The quality of these coaches varies alarmingly. In some you have toilets, some of them have commodes and vanity screens. Some have videos, some magic lanterns. Some lighting, some gas lamps. The impression I'm giving, I hope, is that some are a bit old. The only common denominator is seats, wheels and steward Larry. Larry's task is to open the gates, dish out any credit card purchases, shut the gates and make sure we're all snug and comfy.

His regimen for each journey is to flog as many lottery scratchcards, prize draw tickets and drinks as is humanly possible. To facilitate this he starts selling everything the instant we are clear of The Den gates. In his coffee, tea and cold drinks runs, he, with unerring accuracy, manages to bump into me, even if I'm in a window seat. He also has a policy of putting videos on and then standing in the aisle chatting and blocking the view.

Still he's Millwall through and through and the salt of the earth, so I'll forgive him and his life-time friend, his blue parka. He's roundly abused on every trip, but carries on stoically anyway.

The usual videos on these trips are Millwall "end of season" videos, the odd action film or smutty comedy videos, Mike Reed, Bernard Manning, Jimmy Jones, etc. No Chubby Brown strangely. On one trip we had Jim Davidson's *Sinderella* on video. Even though I'd seen it, I thought it would be a good show to take me dear ol' Mum to see in the West End - us Cockneys love our mother's, you know. She loves him on telly and I thought it would be a good place to go for her 80th birthday. I managed to get tickets for the actual day and very conveniently forgot just how smutty the show was. So, while she loved it, I sat squirming under a barrage of "tit" and "knob" gags.

The most frequent video fodder is *Only Fools And Horses*. For some trips we've had anything up to four hours at a stretch. Just as well it's such "Lovely Jublee" as they say.

Larry has excelled himself on a couple of occasions. On the way home from an "up north" midweek night match, which I believe we lost, he put on *Jungle Book*. Nobody felt very "king of the swingers"-ish, so unfortunately it was met with bewilderment rather than joy.

His masterpiece, however, was when he put on an Arnold Schwartzenegger film, *Red Heat*. Nothing wrong with that you might say, but think about video coach watching:

1) If you're not in the first half a dozen rows you can't see the screen sufficiently, with or without Larry's obstruction.

2) The volume is either at whisper pitch or like a Motorhead concert.

Therefore to put a film on that has the first 20 minutes or so in Russian with subtitles might not be the best choice, do you think?

He also tried to show *Braveheart* on one trip to a coach full of Englishmen. It lasted for the opening credits until he was told to "Take this English hating shit off!", Mel Gibson and Oscars or not, which he did.

Not all coach journeys go smoothly. Some for reasons I've already mentioned, others for more mechanical or traffic reasons. On the way to Wolves in the 90s, we met a mass jam near Birmingham. The police escorted us off the motorway and sped us, sirens blaring, through red lights and up the wrong side of the road. We still got there half an hour late for a 3-3 draw. Incredibly we didn't miss a single goal. Spooky, eh!

The 90s wasn't a good time coach trip wise, as the next three examples admirably show, I think.

BIRMINGHAM CITY: We played Birmingham on a Sunday on an ITV televised live Sunday match in Division One (new). For two consecutive seasons I'd been to 99.99% of games, home and away, except Mickey Mouse "DAF Trophy" affairs, which didn't count! One season I failed to get to Tranmere on Boxing Day, and this season this was my Waterloo.

We set off in good time, but encountered a 20 mile traffic jam on the M1. As you know, "once you're stuck, you're fucked", to quote the RAC. We couldn't leave at an exit until we actually crawled up to one. After what seemed like an eternity, with the kick-off getting ever closer, we managed to get off the M1 and set out "Don't spare the horses – hell for leather" style across country. I don't know if you've been in this situation, but you find yourself rationalising a sort of "chain of events" timetable, which with more optimism than sense, leads you to calculate a predicted arrival just in time for the kick-off and if you're really an optimist will allow you to get a programme and something to eat and drink.

Unfortunately, this is a grand delusion. In the real world in our mad dash - you know the sort of thing, Dracula's coach on the way to the castle to beat the dawn, whip flailing type of thing – the head gasket blew. The fairy tale was over and we limped into a Northamptonshire service station.

"Go on, kick me while I'm down, charge me a fiver for a cup of tea."

"Cha ching."

"Thank you."

We missed the whole game whilst waiting for a replacement coach.

We lost 1-0, but we were all sorry not to get there. As is my wont, I videod any live games for my later delectation. Unfortunately I'd not set the timer correctly and got something like *The Antiques Roadshow* instead. Still, it does say don't kick a man when he's down. It doesn't say anything about bouncing up and down on his head though, does it?

OXFORD UNITED: We drew 3-3 at The Den in a Third Round FA Cup game and we set off to the Manor Ground sure of a win. We were a Division One side at the time –1996 – with Oxford a division below. It was a real pea souper of a night. On the way in, we were handed what you'd call "rainchecks", I suppose, in case of abandonment. If only it had been, we wouldn't have had to watch – what we could see of it – an atrocious performance and a 1-0 defeat.

This game prompted me to write my first and only scathing letter to Millwall Chairman, Peter Mead, enclosing my coach ticket for the next game at Grimsby, and basically informing him that he was the figurehead for a pile of cack masquerading as a football team. This wasn't the only game that prompted this, oh no, but a string of rubbish performances led to me cracking, not helped by . . .

. . . So with bowed heads and mumbled oaths, we boarded our coach for the shortish journey home. We set off on our way and reached the motorway, drove a short distance and some young boys sitting at the back shouted out, "Excuse me, mister, the coach is on fire!"

No response, so they continued their pleas, mostly because it was true. Eventually the driver believed them and we pulled in to the hard shoulder and sat there with lorries and other vehicles rattling us as they sped past. The longer we sat there, or so it seemed, the more things cut out. The radio, the internal lights, heating and finally and more worryingly, the external lights. So we sat there lightless, lifeless and like a bloody big sitting duck, waiting for our replacement coach or for someone to plough into the back of us. Thankfully the coach arrived first.

MIDDLESBROUGH: Thirdly, and by no means least, a trip to Ayresome Park where we never won, not for any match I was at, anyway. So it was this day, for a Division One game in the 90s. We lost 3-0. Miserable enough, you might think – a sound thrashing followed by a six hour coach trip – but we'd not suffered enough, I'm afraid. We left the ground, boarded the coach and the driver said, "Can you give us a push lads?" Yeah right, we all ignored him and carried on what we were doing. It was only after we hadn't moved and he continued this litany that we realised he meant it.

Half of the inhabitants, me included, got off and push started the coach. For some reason this amused the local coppers enormously. They rolled about like Cadbury's *Smash* robots to see such a sight. We told the driver to keep going à la "Speed", whatever happened, as a sound coshing in the game and one coach pushing escapade was enough for one day. Fortunately he obeyed and we got home, albeit late, without further embarrassment.

I've seen and had some peculiar moments on coach trips, like sitting on a coach at Bristol City inside the ground until kick-off as it was chucking it down, and when we dropped a bloke off at the NEC once, Millwall shirted, miles from our preferred route. Still a Lions kit isn't optimum dress in Birmingham, so good luck to him.

We've had various Dutch supporters on coaches, who've travelled over from Holland by ferry, gone to The Den for the coach, gone to the game and then reversed the process to go home the same night. And I thought I was mad!

I encountered one bloke at a service station who used to have his photo taken outside such places. This to me puts train spotters in the shade for sheer pointlessness. "I've not got a shirt on in this picture at Leicester Forest, 'cause I had it taken off my back to pay for some sandwiches." Strange. It could be worse I suppose. He could give us a slide show lecture on the coach home. Service stations of the British Isles. "Mmm, nice!"

One man who is a long standing away traveller once missed the coach at The Den and followed it in his car all the way up the motorway, until we stopped at a services, got out, parked his car, got on the coach, went to the match and did the journey in reverse on the way home.

For one match we came back through Shoreditch and onto Commercial Street, haunt of Jack The Ripper and a notorious red light area. This night it was like *Band Of Gold* or a prossies convention with enough ladies of the night – and it would have to be a very dark night with most of them, I can tell you! – to service the fleet. Unfortunately, as I live north of the river, my request to get off the coach at the bottom of the road was greeted with knowing winks and "We know where you're going!" type cat calls. How preposterous!! You'll hear from my solicitor in the morning!

HARTLEPOOL: As they say, save the best - or in this case the worst – till last. I've been on numerous jaunts "up north" and spent what seems like forever on a coach round trip, but the journey to Hartlepool in 1999/2000 plumbed new depths in Marquis de Sade type pleasures. Foolishly I'd said to Dave and Paul "If one of you drives to The Den, I'll go".

Unfortunately they agreed and off we went. We were on two separate coaches, so I had no way to contact them on the way home. As things panned out, they had no way of knowing if I was going back to the ground for a lift home or if I'd 'phoned The Samaritans and gone straight to a private urgent counselling instead. Someone had decided that this game should be played at noon on a Sunday. Who, I don't know, but thanks anyway. What this meant was that I had to get up at 3.15am. The only saving grace was that the clocks had gone back this night. "Whoopee, an extra hour. That makes four hours kip. Cheers!"

Paul and Dave picked me up at Rotherhithe Tunnel and we arrived at The Den in pitch darkness. The Lions Centre next to the ground was in full swing with an Afro Caribbean "knees up" or "boogie down" or whatever. We'd beat the coach and sat outside until it arrived. It left at 5.00am. Not surprisingly the journey up was easy with no traffic whatsoever, so we sailed up, only stopping when something actually opened. It was very odd riding into a rising sun, very Hammer Horror.

We drove through Hartlepool, which looked quite nice and onto the ground. Even this was quite good, much better than a hell of a lot of others I've seen, that's for sure.

To my surprise a couple of hundred other insomniacs had made the same masochistic trip. One thing we did notice on the way up was that the southbound carriageway was like a traffic cone storage depot. Still, more of that later.

Sitting behind us in the stand was Tim Carter. This will mean nothing to anyone else, but he was Millwall's ex-keeper. At this game the home team had decided to unveil "H'Angus" the monkey mascot, based on their Napoleonic spy hanging exploits in years gone by. I could have cheerfully hung him myself at the end. Someone behind me said "You northerners are strange. If we get a monkey, we spend it. If you lot get one, you hang it!" A bit of cultural difference observation there. See old episodes of *Minder* for a Cockney explanation, if required.

As I've previously mentioned, the game was played in a gale and we lost 1-0 in the last minute to a goal from a non-existent corner, which, wind and referee assisted, they managed to get into our net, right in front of us. Marvellous. As the rest of the country was now awake, the usual Sunday driver phenomenon was in full swing. The traffic on the motorway had built up alarmingly. We seemed to drift from one massive cone induced traffic jam to the next. I got the impression that practically the entire M1 had roadworks as we edged along at a snail's pace.

The only video we had on the coach was one that someone just happened to have with him. It had the previous night's *Match Of The Day*, which passed an hour or so. It then went into channel hopping around cable stations for the rest of the tape. If you've got cable, you'll know what sort of tosh we were watching, albeit fleetingly. QVC, UK Gold, TNT, Bravo. All top notch stuff. If it had stayed on one channel, it might have been tolerable, but this was view a few seconds of each then switch to next channel. This was the equivalent of audio visual torture. Very similar to what Alex in *A Clockwork Orange* endures, except this made me feel more violent, not less. Put it this way, if I'd had a gun I'd have used it first on the video, then on myself. It would have been a mercy, I can assure you. We eventually reached the outskirts of London and hit every single set of traffic lights on red. When we got to Highbury Corner we hit a diversion and more roadworks.

What made the situation worse was that I'd arranged to meet four mates in a pub in Bethnal Green on the assumption I'd be home in time. I got off the coach at Shoreditch and walked to the pub in a daze. Just as one of my mates Keith was calling my mobile to see where I was, I was pushing the pub door open at about 9.30pm. None of them had seen me like this, as I think I had post traumatic stress. I babbled incoherently, had a couple of rapid fire pints which didn't touch the sides, and gradually calmed down to my usual unintelligible babble.

In all my years man and boy, this is the worst trip I've ever been on. 13 hours in the saddle with sensory torture thrown in for good measure. Never again!! Add in a few more hours to this and I could fly to Australia. That puts it in context, I think.

Right, what's the next away match?

CHAPTER 17

GREAT RAILWAY JOURNEYS OF THE WORLD

TRANS-SIBERIAN RAILWAYS? Pah! These people should have travelled on football specials. That's hardship, I can tell you.
The usual state of play was to give you the most decrepit rolling stock (or non-rolling in some cases) available. "The train's been delayed, I'm afraid, we've got to get the cattle off first and sweep the straw and cow shit out!" Sadly not far from the truth. Such namby pamby things like lights and heat were deemed an unnecessary extravagance on many trips and for Millwall organised buffets in our First Division days, it was obligatory to try and out-do the motorway services in the "stripe-up" stakes.

I believe the drivers also have instructions to stop as close to any muck spreading work as possible, so that we Londoners could get a real taste and smell of the countryside. A sort of field (of shit) trip, I suppose. Trainspotters, well what can you say, sad or what. In many train trips up north when passing their massed ranks at Crewe it was de rigueur to roundly abuse these woeful creatures and, if possible, to pelt them with tins of drink, preferably full. Once the railway twigged this, they moved us to a middle rail out of range.

If you're not up on trainspotting, it's not a clip board, pen and pad. Oh no! It's hi-tech surveillance gear, AWACs in the air tracking a train's progress, video cameras, mobile 'phones, mini discs to record every "chigadee boom" as the train goes past, radar and satellite link-ups via the internet. They use enough equipment to hunt for Red October, let alone the 8.57 from Cheadle Hulme. Sad, very, very sad, but at least state of the art.

A friend of mine, Keith, went up to Cumbria on a steam train with some work mates. His mission: to drink copious amounts of real ale. On this train some people recorded and videoed the whole journey. This should make you very wary of "Why don't you pop round?" invites, as you may find yourself in the company of a rail enthusiast, resplendent in guard's uniform, whistle and flag, armed with six hours of audio and video torture, in the form of his recorded trips to the Western Highlands on The Flying Scotsman. Beware!

On post "specials" train journeys, Millwall would book up X amount of seats in the name of Mr Neil, Billy Neil, ex-Millwall player,

114

and away travel co-ordinator. On one such trip, we encountered a creature who for sheer pointlessness of hobby was unsurpassed. As you probably know when you book seats in advance on a train, a card with seat number, destination, and name is stuck to the back of the relevant seat. On this particular trip we had 50 or so seats in one carriage.

We stopped somewhere in the Midlands and quite a lot of "normal" people got off. Out came this man who began gathering up the old reservation tickets from the back of the seats just vacated. We looked at him warily and he said, "I collect these tickets, it's my hobby. I expect you think I'm strange." Good Lord, no!

It was also customary to slow trains up to avoid rival fans arriving at London termini at the same time. We did this many times successfully, but one time we pulled into Euston alongside a train of London "Scousers". The look on their faces when they saw a train load of Millwall pulling up the side of them was priceless. Cue mass outbreak of singing as soon as you get off. Marvellous acoustics, stations!

I thought I'd run through some of the more incident filled journeys, just to give you a flavour of the joys of rail travel. Pity it isn't still the age of steam, then you could get buggered about and get a face full of soot into the bargain.

MIDDLESBROUGH: I foolishly went on a stag night the evening before a trip to Middlesbrough, got in about 4.00am "soused to the gunwales" and had to get up at 8.00am to get the train to Thornaby on a club special. Apart from the fact that I just wished someone would shoot me to put me out of my misery, the trip was fairly uneventful, save for a prolonged "muck spreading" stop, guaranteed to clear your tubes, but not particularly high on the priority list the night after a skinful, I can tell you. The main reason for its inclusion was that the train was like something out of an Agatha Christie novel with wooden individual carriages, "Murder on the Orient (Millwall) Express", complete with fat Belgian sleuth type of thing. It was good of BR to excel itself, as it must have been a real treat for railway enthusiasts, actually being able to travel on a working museum.

PORTSMOUTH: This was a self inflicted problem, I'm afraid. I'm a Londoner so naturally I believe that all trains go to London. Arrogance, of course, but if "all roads lead to Rome", then "all trains must go to London" in my logic. Jim Stephenson, my travelling companion on this trip and I went to Fratton Park in the 90s. After the game we went back to the station and I persuaded him to get on any train, as they "all go to London". We seemed to stop everywhere and nowhere I recognised. When it stopped at Chichester, it began to dawn on me that my initial assumption may not be strictly accurate, as the train was in fact going to Brighton, so we disembarked there and got a train back to Victoria. I believe this game was a 6-1 defeat and the culmination of the "Rioch out!" campaign, so it was a thoroughly good day all round.

VARIOUS: On other trips I've taken over two hours to do an hour's journey from Reading and only just arrived at Paddington in time to catch the last train to Whitechapel. We came back on a train from Newcastle, which featured the least well disguised Geordie hooligan "reccy" ever. There was no actual trouble, but it was a bit obvious, canny lad!

A general note and one that usually holds true in the main, the better the train the less people are inclined to abuse it. Give people cattle trucks and "beat up" carriages, they will usually be left like a pig sty and get the treatment they probably deserve. I suppose I can understand why the railway companies don't give football fans, well Millwall anyway, decent rolling stock. It's because in the 60s and 70s train carriages were re-arranged on a regular basis with the fans aboard carrying out their own brand of interior decorating by slashing the seats, ripping out the fittings and smashing all the windows. In truth, apart from minor stuff, I've only seen minimal damage to any Millwall train I've been on. Somebody threw one of the tables out once and we've had many a trainee fireman in our midst setting off the fire extinguishers, but that's all, believe it or not.

LEICESTER CITY: A trip by train to Leicester, one of the more volatile grounds, means that you encounter a number of interesting points. Firstly you pass by a park called Nelson Mandela Park, very Del Boy and all that. Perhaps Leicester's twinned with Peckham? If escorted you have to march up the side of a motorway and under several crossing bridges, lovely place for an ambush (surprisingly it's not happened yet) and you also pass a prison that looks like a castle. Just thought I'd share this information with you.

I travelled to Leicester with Jim on the train with the London branch of the Leicester City Supporters Club, when there was an away fan embargo due to stand building. We lost 4-0. Me and Jim sat in the home stand behind the goal and tried to be discrete. Unfortunately as we got stuffed we had no cause to be otherwise.

There were actually quite a few "undercover" Millwall there, but one man who most definitely blew his cover was a Millwall fan who used to come from St Albans for home and away games. He was standing on Leicester station in a Millwall shirt. I think the locals' consensus was that he was a "care in the community" case and best left alone.

WEST BROMWICH ALBION: We went to West Brom in the 90s and the train pulled up some way outside the station and sat there motionless by a grass embankment. After a while some people said "Sod this! I'm going down the slope!" Quite a few decided that this was a good idea and opened the doors and scampered down the grassy slope. Some reached the bottom and some halfway when the train slowly started to move. This prompted a charge back up the slope in an effort to re-board the train. What ensued was like a scene from a Western, with train doors open and the train's occupants trying to haul the stragglers back on board. Some didn't make it. I presume the Indians got them.

SOUTHAMPTON: In 1986 we played Southampton in a Fifth Round FA Cup tie. Me and Steve K went to this game on a club special. Millwall had decided that in an effort to contain the travelling hordes, they would only allow you to buy a train ticket and not give you a match ticket until you got on the train. We took five trains and each train had a different colour ticket to identify it. With military efficiency this plan worked – going anyway. We drew 0-0 and lost the replay at home. This particular season we played Southampton in both cups, the same as we had played Chelsea the season prior.

As I said, this plan worked marvellously going. What the tacticians behind this strategy hadn't thought of was the return journey. It was quite easy to stagger "colour coded" trains from Waterloo, but a different matter at Southampton. Consequently 4,000 away fans arrive at the station at the same time with the intention of boarding the first train out. What occurred was mayhem – windows smashed, surges, and general chaos. Steve and I were in disagreement about the best strategy, but I said I'm going on a later train, not being too keen on the "last train out of Bombay, hang from the rafters" scenario that I envisaged. I boarded a later train and in a tactic I've previously mentioned, the train took an "all over the shop" route to stagger our arrival.

This was the night Barry McGuigan fought Carlos Pedrosa at QPR for the world title and I only just managed to get in to watch it on ITV. Just thought I'd mention it.

MANCHESTER UNITED: The two visits in our two top flight seasons, both hidings 3-0 and 5-1, were both interesting trips. As you can imagine, we took a large following to both of these games with several trains. The first season the northbound trip to Warwick Road was uneventful, but the return trip south was a nightmare. The police held us at the station until after 7.00pm, ostensibly because earlier trains had been bricked, so when we got on the train the police told us to pull the blinds down to avoid any missiles. Nothing happened. Several people on the train in high spirits set off a fire extinguisher and also decided to chuck their mate's coat off the train as we passed through Crewe. Unfortunately his wallet, keys, money etc went with it.

The train adopted the "World Tour" tactic and we, Micky, Steve and I got back to the East End too late for the pub, so we had to go into a local Chinese restaurant to get a drink. Drastic times require drastic measures.

For the second visit we didn't arrive until 2.50pm, got frog marched up the road and got into the ground just in time to see the kick-off. We scored first, which must have upset them, as they then proceeded to thrash us within an inch of our life.

I went on my own for this trip, my only companion being Stephen King's *Misery*, which I found at Coventry some weeks prior. Very apt, I'm sure you'll agree. The train home left promptly, but we had no heating or lighting for 90% of the trip. Still some people pay good money for sensory deprivation of this standard.

BLACKBURN ROVERS: It was customary at Blackburn for the police to escort the away fans to a local pub for some unknown reason. There was never any trouble, so I suppose it wasn't a bad idea. On one trip in the early 90s, pre Jack Walker funded glory, I went on a very long train to Blackburn. The train stopped outside the station, or so we thought. We sat in the rear carriages waiting for the train to pull in when a startled looking train guard came into our carriage and in a remarkable "George Formbyesque" accent said "What are you lot doing here? T'train's bin in t'station for ten minutes!"

Scenario: Long train plus short platform plus thick Londoners equals confusion.

We followed him through the train to where the platform was, got outside and saw the rest of our fans disappearing into the distance, heading to the pub. As the buck-toothed ukelele plucker might have said, "Turned out shite again."

NEWCASTLE UNITED: In 1992 Jim and I went to Newcastle for the "freezing your nuts off" game that I've previously mentioned. This was the Sunday before Christmas and Jim had got cheap tickets, which were still about £50. I arrived at Kings Cross in good time and waited. Jim was late, so I thought I'd start to queue up. What I didn't know was that I should have got a boarding pass. As I'm not psychic and it hadn't been mentioned anywhere, how was I supposed to know? I'd been queuing for about half an hour and Jim still hadn't shown with the 9.00am departure time rapidly approaching. Luckily as this was Christmas time, the train had been delayed to put extra carriages on.

Jim arrived and we reached the ticket barrier without said passes. The ticket Nazi lambasted me for not having a pass and intimated that he wouldn't let me on unless I got a pass and stopped arguing with him. I did point out to him that if I didn't get on after paying £50, I would take out retribution on his gonads. He saw the logic in my reasoning and let me on.

The trip took five hours, it was absolutely freezing and we drew 1-1, with Newcastle being awarded the most dubious home crowd inspired penalty I've ever seen. After the game the police took the train travellers back to the station in the back of Black Marias, sirens blaring, through red lights and the wrong way up one way streets. Jolly exciting it was too.

NOTTS COUNTY: I went up to Nottingham with Simon and another sometime companion, Dave (yes, another Dave). We played cards and Simon and Dave had a smoke, I'm not talking Embassy No1s here, more the old bootleg Marlboros as we used to call them. A bit more inclined towards Amsterdam's usual fare, if you get my drift. I sat there on sentry duty, fully alert (I don't smoke) on look out for the inspector to spring us, trying to break as many train regulations as possible at one time - gambling, smoking in a no smoking compartment, and for your smoking matter to be of the "Cheech and Chong" variety. Disgraceful.

The first away match of the 2000/2001 season saw us again play at Notts County, a ground I've been to seven times, and including this 4-3 win, I've seen six wins and just one defeat. Simon and Pat were on holiday, so Paul, Nathan and I gathered at St Pancras to get a mid-morning train up to Nottingham. Usually if we go by train, Simon gets cheap tickets for us all on his family railcard, but as he was away we didn't have this luxury, so I walked up to the ticket office and uttered the immortal line, "A return to Nottingham, please."

"£41, please."

"No, madam, I only want one."

"That is one, sir."

I then had a fit of the vapours in shock, and had to have the smelling salts thrust under my nose. Not strictly true, but they certainly know how to charge don't they!

The trip up was uneventful and we sat in the stand not expecting Mad Ted to appear, when as if by magic, he did. He'd been at Edgbaston watching Warwickshire v Middlesex in the County Championship, but managed to navigate his way to Nottingham.

As I mentioned earlier, the PA announcer had whistling dentures. Always an ice breaker. We cruised to a 3-0 lead, got pegged back to 3-3, and scored a screamer in the last minute to win 4-3. Wonderful.

We walked back to the station, we boarded our train and headed south, only to stop at Leicester whilst another train load of people got on. We sat there and sat there and as usual no news was forthcoming regarding the cause of the delay. We only found out that someone had thrown themselves under a train further up the line when another batch of passengers got on.

What this meant was that our train had to go back northwards to Nottingham to come south again as the southbound line was closed due to the gore. This added an hour to our return journey. So business as usual then.

BRIGHTON: For one of our jaunts to the seaside, I went with Jim. At this time he had a rail card and also some vouchers which enabled us to sit in the First Class compartment for a normal fare. We took up our seats in the luxurious compartment and we were confronted by a particularly stroppy copper, who couldn't comprehend the idea that two common as muck Millwall fans could possibly sit in the posh section. It took a while to convince him that we had the correct paperwork and we gained no small amount of satisfaction when our Gestapo-like interrogator admitted defeat and begrudgingly left us in peace.

For some trains there seems to be a ploy with their First Class section. What would appear to be the policy is this: Put about two or three normal carriages on and about ten First Class carriages, the thinking being that people will pay the extra dosh rather than stand up in the aisle for a couple of hundred miles. Usually this doesn't work and the compartment ends up being crammed to the gills or has people walking up and down to find a seat the whole journey. Greedy buggers.

PETERBOROUGH: I went to a night match again with Jim, this time to Peterborough. For this journey Jim had left half his ticket at home so only had the return portion. When the ticket inspector came around we had a long drawn out "chat" about the situation. We said to him he could check with the credit card company, as this is how Jim had booked the tickets, and in any case why would you have a return portion of a ticket if you were travelling in the opposite direction? Not very plausible, we said. It wouldn't wash with our Asian jobsworth and I got quite wound-up with the whole situation, so much so that the inspector went away to get a plain clothes policeman to bring us in to line.

I still argued with him along the same lines and I would have thought I was quite close to being either nicked or thrown off the train when we came to an agreement and he let us go on. It was at Peterborough that I saw Millwall miss a ridiculous amount of chances in one game which ended 0-0 and consisted of our forwards adopting the old "couldn't hit a horse's arse with a cricket bat" principle. It could have been a cricket score. "Funny old game, Saint," as they say.

It was on the return trip from Peterborough that we had kids running amok on the train wrecking the toilet, spreading toilet paper the length of the carriage and setting off the fire extinguishers. This was a "new" train carriage, so bang goes my earlier "behaviour" theory.

GRIMSBY: On one trip to Grimsby for a 0-0 game on a Sunday in one of our previous play-off seasons in May, 1994, we travelled up by train to sunny Cleethorpes. It was the last game of the season and we were massed in the away stand.

At the end of the game we were greeted by hundreds of locals on the pitch, presumably wishing us well. I assume that's what the offer to join them on the pitch meant. As we had an eight foot fence in front of us, we declined their kind invite and left the ground, we walked up to Cleethorpes station, got the train, sat down and were joined by a very twitchy squaddy on his way back to his barracks. He was quite friendly, but seemed to be on a short fuse. So there's

121

me envisaging a couple of hundred mile return trip with one of Her Majesty's trained killers for company. Lovely. Luckily his stop came up quite quickly and he got off.

SHEFFIELD WEDNESDAY: Finally the trip to hell. We played at Sheffield in the old Division One on the 3rd of February, 1990. I went on my own for this trip and I boarded the club special train at St Pancras at about 10.00am. It was another cold day. "What in England? Surely not."

As we got to Luton it was snowing and the train ground to a halt and rumours of engine trouble started circulating. They changed the locomotive and off we went, but slower than we should. It stopped again, several times in fact. It was pretty obvious that all was not well. I believe they again changed engines, but put a slower, less powerful one on. As a bi-product of all this we had no heat on board and it was a bit parky. Where's "Damart" when you need them?

We eventually arrived at Leicester some time after 2.00pm. It was obvious to us all that we weren't going to make it in time. We asked if we could just turn around and go back to London. No response. There wasn't a buffet on the train and as it was Milwall, it was a "dry" train, i.e. alcohol free. Quite a few people got off at Leicester and like a swarm of locust ransacked the station buffet / off licence. People armed with goodies got back on board and the train continued northwards on its relentless trek. We pulled up at Chesterfield station to be met by a platform of police and police dogs. They were all rolling about "laughing policeman" style at our plight. I always remember this when you want public assistance, chaps.

We arrived at Wadsley Bridge, Sheffield at about 4.30pm. It's about a 20 minute walk to the ground, so it was announced it was naturally too late to go to the game and we did a circle around Sheffield and headed towards London. The phrase "Told you so" springs to mind.

We got back to St Pancras at about 7.30 – 8.00 pm. Strangely much quicker coming back than going. We promptly laid siege to the ticket office demanding a refund. "Get it from your club," we were told.

As Millwall fans aren't renowned for their patience, miraculously the station remained unwrecked. I took my ticket back to Millwall the next week and in an act that shows my mentality, I bought a ticket for the next away match with the refund.

CHAPTER 18

FLAT CAPS AND WHIPPETS – UP NORTH

IN THE TOP three divisions, I've been to every ground except Leeds and Bradford, so I've had numerous reasons to travel up north and I can confirm that in some instances it is, in fact, grim up there. Some places are really quite nice, while others are like a recession inspired bomb site. It's just like London in reality. London's streets aren't all paved with gold, more like shop door sleeping homeless, beggars, and wandering Albanian asylum seekers complete with pity inducing small children. That's the reality, but where would we be without a few generalisations?

Apart from the trips I've mentioned elsewhere, a few more do stand out.

BLACKPOOL: I'd been to Blackpool on a beano not long before this trip and a bloody good weekend it was too. This was my first football trip. In January, 1997, I went up on a club coach with Jim.

At this time Millwall were in grave financial straits and were in real danger of going out of business. I got a creditor's report, as I'm a shareholder, and it was so thick I thought it was a new telephone directory. It was rumoured that this game may actually be our last ever game.

About 1,500 went to this game to witness what in my opinion was one of our worst ever away performances, a 3-0 defeat against fairly poor opposition. Better to go out with a whimper than a bang though, eh lads? On the coach trip up we seemed to have some minor problems with the front door mechanism, but this didn't stop us from getting to Blackpool very early. On entering the ground it became apparent that Bloomfield Road looked a lot better from the top of Blackpool Tower than it did up close.

We stood on a ramshackle open terrace and that's being complimentary. I doubt this ground had seen a lick of paint since Stanley Matthews R.I.P. was a lad. After the game we trudged out disconsolately wondering if this load of tosh would be our last abiding memory or if Millwall did in fact still have a future. We set off home and the door was still playing up. The driver pulled into the nearest services in an effort to repair it. Quite why he didn't fix it in the three hours we were in the ground, you'd better ask him because I'm buggered if I know. Jim and I got off and were told it would only be a short break, so not to stray too far. Two hours later we were still standing there like lemons, waiting for a replacement coach as our original one was deemed unroadworthy. We eventually got back to London's Victoria station in time for Jim to get the last train home and for me to get the last tube.

Why is it that some drivers <u>have</u> to go via the coach station at Victoria? One of life's great mysteries, I think.

THE GRIM PLACES: Rotherham near the ground looks like one huge rusty scrap yard. Coal mines and old satanic mills, slag heaps, chimneys pumping out God knows what in to the air. Your umbrella's no good against acid rain, old boy!

Parts of Barnsley, the Lebanon style parts of Liverpool, Blackburn's T.S. Lowry red bricked Coronation Streets. After one game there I remember the home fans trudging home, brow beaten with faces looking like people who'd just had their whippet kicked, their pigeon loft burnt down, and their dominoes stolen. Cheer up you buggers, you won!

Grimsby (Cleethorpes) – such a romantic name. Smells like a fishmongers. Enough said.

Birmingham, not north for every one, but it is for us, arrgh!

Chesterfield's crooked spire, what's all that about, were the plans folded? Quite a lot of places up north look like Dagenham, which if you've ever been there is no compliment.

Obviously London is absolutely perfect, so I'm in a strong position to make sweeping generalisations.

BURY: We went up to Bury for an end of season game a few seasons ago, on the day they won the Division Championship. Jim, Glyn, another away regular and myself went up on a cheap day return on a designated train. We got the metro from Piccadilly station through Manchester and walked to the ground. Bury's a nice suburban type place as far as I could see. We lost the match and for the first time ever we got applauded out of the ground by the delirious home fans. Whether it's because we were crap and gave them the points or because they thought us jolly nice chaps, I don't know.

We went back to Manchester via the metro, but as our train didn't leave until 8.00pm, we decided to go to the station bar, which seemed preferable to chancing our arm in a strange pub in the town centre. So Glyn and I had a drink or several, Jim doesn't drink! But his teeth have all rotted due to massive coke intake - Coca-Cola, not the old Peruvian marching powder. Just kidding. In the bar we got talking to a Man City fan pre hostilities as we had common ground discussing the merits, or lack of them, of our two teams. We eventually got our train and Glyn and I decided we weren't comatose enough yet and carried on drinking all the way home. Jim doesn't drink! Doesn't drink! Did I mention that?

MAN CITY: I've been here several times as previously listed. My main reason for mentioning them again was quite what their "big fish in a very small pond" season in our Division meant to their fans. A lot of the grounds in Division Two are less than salubrious to say the least. You'd certainly have no illusions of how low you'd slumped when you visit some of the following – Luton with its claustrophobic, restricted view away end and its patio-cum-garden centre style executive boxes, Wrexham's three sides and a derelict pub, Fulham's derelict, quaint piece of riverside luxury, Macclesfield, which is too bizarre to go into again, Wigan's Springfield Park. Well what can you say? The palatial splendour that is Gillingham, Blackpool, Colchester, Chesterfield and Bristol Rovers. The Walsall "B&Q Superstore" ground. It's just fortunate they got out before having to sample the academic delights of Oxford and Cambridge otherwise their perception of their lofty status would have crashed to Earth with a bump.

SCUNTHORPE: My only visit to Scunthorpe was in 1999 for a fantastic 4-1 win. It's another Walsall / Northampton pre-fabricated type of ground. We tried to get coach tickets for this game and were told that they'd sold out. This was before one of our home games. We decided to go and check out if they were going to add any more coaches after the game and very foolishly decided to employ Mad Ted's diplomatic skills to find out. He insulted everyone behind the away travel window and left us, by association, in a situation of possibly being banned from our own away travel. I did point out that "F-ing people up hills and down dales" wasn't the best tactic in getting them on your side. "He's just called me a fucking cunt. I must lay on transport for him." You get the picture.

We were rescued by the people who run the Junior Lions coaches, who said they had a few places left. They were dubious of taking Ted, but in the end he was as good as gold on the trip. We travelled up with the juniors which consisted of about 12 kids and 36 blokes. It was a breath of fresh air with free magazines, videos to watch, quizzes for the kids, and sweets for all.

In the ground we were given our own stand behind the goal. Before the game, which we got to quite early, I noticed a ball lodged behind a seat in front of us. We went down and got it and found it was a brand new official Nationwide League ball. Being honest chaps, we stuck it up our coat and smuggled it back on to the coach with us.

For most "normal" away games the usual away following is the 500 or so same faces. For the more volatile games, the "boys" swell this number and so it was for this game with a 250 strong firm turning up. We were right next to the home fans' meathead community and a very homely looking bunch they were too. One particularly "Scunny" with no shirt, or hair come to that, tried to get into our end - not advisable, I wouldn't have thought – and had to be restrained by about half a dozen stewards.

Towards the end of the rout, the home "boys" exited the ground and Millwall's mob tried to do likewise, but were locked in, thus delaying the "off". I suppose it did happen, but I had to get back on the coach to finish the "beano", so I didn't hang about. At Swiss Cottage the team coach caught us up, prompting much waving and cheering. On some previous occasions this has happened after away defeats when fist waving and mouthed oaths weren't quite so welcome.

NEWCASTLE: At Newcastle, a venue where for one game a party travelled up by aeroplane. Something I've not done, but knowing my luck it would end up like an *Airport* film style disaster movie. The local police usually give you a letter on the way in, telling you what's expected of you. It's another "hot bed" ground and can be hostile inside and outside. As I've already mentioned, at the brass monkeys Christmas time game in 1992 the crowd's persuasive powers were shown in all their glory when largely thanks to the crowd cajoling the referee's assistant, the referee awarded the most dubious penalty I've ever seen. The "linesman" showed the usual stock resistance and stuck his flag up immediately the Geordies started baying.

SHEFFIELD UNITED: The away stand is not an ideal spot for vertigo sufferers, in fact the half time entertainment could have Eddie Edwards doing ski jumps. Sadly head first into the pitch knowing his talent. But the stand is very, very steep and is more suited to sherpas than us flatland Londoners.

SHEFFIELD WEDNESDAY: This ground in more modern times is the home of the brass band accompaniment to "Barmy Army!" chants, former home of Big Ron, the man with his own language, and the bald beer bellied Buddha bloke. This ground on my various visits - all defeats - has to my mind the largest "Kop" style home stand in the League. It used to be open to the skies with no roof. They must breed them tough in the land of *The Full Monty*. They must have had to tie themselves to the crush barriers on more breezy days on t'moors and probably had a mountain rescue team complete with St Bernards on standby. A bit chilly for me, I'm afraid.

BARNSLEY: A very schizophrenic place with shut down pits, nutty slack and posh houses. It's a ground, however, with a very good disabled facility with a Heidi style chalet perched above and to the right hand side of the away terrace, when I was there a few years ago anyway. I've not seen the new renovated ground. I've seen Millwall play here about five times and never lose. It's the only ground where I've actually been ushered to my correct seat, like being in the cinema, for my first visit, a 2-1 win. It had no atmosphere whatsoever for any visit I've had and seemed to be full of bluff Yorkshire folk. Bloody good pies, though, ground of our Arthur Scargill piss takes and for my first visit the local police warned us about a probable bricking on our way home. We pulled the blinds down, but nothing happened, happen!

STOCKPORT: My only visit so far ended in a 5-1 defeat with an ageing Ray Wilkins in tow. There must be a certain amount of local pride because my mates Keith and Steve were at a beer festival and spoke to a northern bloke and insulted him by saying he came from Manchester and he proudly informed them he was from Stockport actually! I'm all for local pride - "I'm not from London, i'm from Stepney actually!"

In a similar vein, I'm in a band who were playing a gig in Lewisham. At the interval a bloke who'd been dancing away around the pool table during our first set came up to me and started complimenting us. He looked northern, like a squaddy on twitch alert and completely out of the blue announced "I'm from Manchester!"

We all looked at him blankly. We were mulling over our options:
1) Beat the shit out of him, as you would do

2) Burst into a round of enthusiastic applause in admiration or

3) Give him a rousing chorus of "For he's a jolly good fellow!", finishing with three hearty "Hip, hip, hoorays!"

A very unnecessary bit of information, I thought, but thanks. "I'm mad for it." And so was he, I'd imagine.

YORK: I've been to the historic city of York only once so far, for football anyway, in 1989 with Steve K. As I've previously mentioned, we'd left London in reasonable temperatures and had driven all the way with the heater on and didn't stop until we came to a junction signalling "York" or "Leeds". We got out to check the right way and were both given a good old Yorkshire welcome as a freezing wind chilled us to the bone. We quickly got back in the car with the sound of chattering teeth drowning out the radio. When we got to the ground we were very glad to find a lovely open air terrace. Cheers.

BOLTON: This was another incident packed trip, in my one and only visit to Burnden Park for a 4-0 defeat in Division 1 in 1993. Simon, Jim, and the two Daves went up with me on the train via Wigan shuttle service. Our first port of call was the chip shop and then the pub, which I've mentioned in previous chapters. After the drink we walked up to the ground and took up our position on a side terrace to the left of the odd supermarket filled goal end terrace. The home fans were really getting behind their team. Quite right as well. We had the sun in our eyes the whole game. Just as well as it turned out, as we capitulated alarmingly.

It was one of those games when a former player comes back to haunt you, in this case John McGinlay. We demanded a steward's inquiry when the player we thought Dobbinish suddenly became Red Rum. We did think about leaving early – "What, and miss another nail in my heart goal? No thanks."

So we decided to suffer the slaughter manfully to the bitter end. We went back to the local station and again caught the shuttle, but this time to Manchester Piccadilly. A couple of local northern lasses, I think the expression is, sat opposite us and we "entertained" them with our dazzling London charm. We gave them our best "up north" impressions. You know, "You alright chuck, eh up! Jack, put wood in t'hole, Lancashire hot pot" sort of thing. Amazingly they seemed to find us amusing and we had a good laugh.

When we got to Manchester station, we found a porter - not Gail Porter sadly! – and asked what platform the first London train was leaving from. He told us a number and pointed in the general direction. We headed off and found a train about to go, so we jumped aboard. We were a bit surprised to find it was packed. We managed to find seats and a table and sat down. It gradually dawned on us that this was in fact a Tottenham "special", coming back from United or City, I know not which. Anyway we sat there reading our programmes and playing cards. Not surprisingly our reading matter bore no resemblance to theirs.

A few odd things struck us. This train had lights and . . . heat! Heat? It was like a Mangrove swamp! This stunned us into awed silence as it was not what we were used to. Wot no cattle trucks, not cold, dark or starved of food and drink style transport for London's elite? Oh no! At Euston we were accosted by a Tottenham club official, who informed us we were banned for life from travelling with Spurs away travel. As you can imagine, this left us mortified, distraught and uncontrollably sobbing.

1999-2000 NORTHERN TOUR: At the end of last season our run-in consisted of two consecutive Saturday trips to the far north and then an additional midweek game in the play-off semi finals, making three 500 mile round trips in just over three weeks. Our itinerary:

BURNLEY: My third visit to the enigma that is Burnley. "Will the real Royston Veysey please stand up?!" This time for our trek to Turf Moor, me and the usual suspects Simon, Paul, Nathan, Mad Ted and the two Daves (Simms and Murray) took the club coach via a more direct route to *The League Of Gentlemen* world that is Burnley. We had just over 2,000 fans in a stand behind the goal, outplayed the home side, and found ourselves 4-0 down within an hour. This prompted a fight-back of Herculean proportions where save for the woodwork, a blatant penalty declined, goal line clearances and blind luck on the home side's behalf, our eventual defeat, 4-3, would have resulted in a win for us if the clock hadn't been against us. Such was the sheer panic our resurgence had instilled in the home defence.

It also gave us an opportunity to renew our acquaintance with the multiple talent, footballer, thespian, rap star, chat show host and more prestigiously star of "Chicken Tonight" ads that is Ian Wright. The warm greeting he received would, I'm sure, have gladdened his heart.

As we sat and stood on board our coach waiting for it to leave, we exchanged the usual niceties with the home fans passing us in the street, in a great football tradition. As the menagerie of northern humanity passed, one woman flashed us. I'm a bit shy, so I couldn't bring myself to look, I'm afraid. (It was a black lacy Wonderbra 36C, oops what a giveaway!)

PRESTON: The following Saturday another 8.00am(ish) coach, on my own this time to Champions elect Preston, to witness their celebrations and the most inept refereeing display I have ever seen and believe me, that is saying something. But don't take my word for it, as *The Sun* also said so and they hate us. So there.

I stood on a side terrace behind the dug-outs and feasted my eyes on the re-vamped splendour that is Deepdale. Since my only other visit, Bill Shankly has had his head deified on a stand as well. This game was a sell-out and for the home side at least was a balloon hoisting, flag waving, "Campione, Campione olé olé olé!" knees up day. For us it was a vital clash in an effort to get into the second automatic spot.

Prior to the game we had music played at us at ear splitting volume and had *Nissan Doormat* sung at us by slimboy tenor, Russell Watson. We sang all the way through it. Sod culture! Still, Pavarotti after winning Slimmer Of The Year does nothing for me I'm afraid.

The game was "refereed" (sic) by a complete cunt. Sorry, no other word for it I'm afraid. He booked practically every Millwall player, turned down the most obvious penalty I've ever seen bar none (which would have made it 1-1), and gave every 50-50 decision to the home side. He even tried to send off Millwall's subs who were warming up, leaving usually mild mannered Nigel Spinks having to be calmed by his assistants. Once again we went behind, this time 3-0, and once again we fought back and once again came within an ace of getting a result.

In this game Preston had Michael Jackson and more worryingly, Paul McKenna, in their squad. The latter may explain the ref's total bias and incompetence as he may have hypnotised him into performing like a complete twat prior to the game, who knows. We lost 3-2 and had a run-in with the local constabulary resplendent in riot gear, whilst throwing pies and coins at the locals. Still the ref had done his job and our automatic slot was fast disappearing. Just a tip, when you ref a Millwall game in the future, it may be easier to write all of Millwall's team in your book first and just tick them off when you caution them. I'm sure this will add to your efficiency and leave you more time to be more creative in your home flavoured decision making.

WIGAN: Somehow we managed to get into the play-off semis via a last day reprieve with Bristol Rovers and Stoke shooting themselves in the foot, and so it was we met our nemesis, Wigan, over two legs. We drew 0-0 at The Den in a drab game. We set off up north, the usual crew plus Simon's son Patrick, Clive, a home regular, and Dave's mate Trevor. We drove up in our mini bus. On arrival at the splendid JJB Stadium, I bumped into my cousins, Paul and Gavin, outside and we commented on the huge police presence, but more of that later.

We had 3,000 to 4,000 fans up there and we occupied a side stand, with the home fans barely filling the two stands they did occupy and with one end completely empty. What with this and Wigan's abysmal turn out at The New Den, I don't believe that they as a town deserve success, but that's my opinion.

In the great Millwall tradition I could have written a report of the evening's events days prior, so predictable was the outcome. It would have gone something like this:

1) Wigan will have very little support.

2) We will take a huge following and make a huge row.

3) The police will deploy their entire force armed to the teeth.

4) Millwall will dominate totally, miss a hatful of chances and concede a dubious goal late on.

5) The police will instigate trouble if it appears unlikely to start of its own accord.

And lo, in true Nostradamus fashion, so it was. We massed in the stand, sang all night, displayed our huge St George flag, were personally applauded by our Chairman, did indeed dominate and as sure as night follows day, lost to a soft own goal conceded from a dubious free kick. Was it ever any other way.

The team couldn't really have done much more. However . . .

The real fun was the police. As I mentioned previously, the turn out by the "boys in blue" was impressive with *Robocop* style riot police in full body armour, dogs, horses, hundreds of officers, banks of video camera wielding plod, and save for the police motor cycle display team, we were treated to all that Lancashire's finest could muster. A good night to be out with the stripey jumper, mask and swag bag, I'd say.

Clive doesn't go to many out of London away games and so wasn't privy to the likely police tactics as I was. He couldn't believe this show of force, with many officers openly carrying CS gas during the game, where save for our usual exuberant support, nothing was going on. The police deployed riot police the entire length of our side stand (the length of the pitch), two to three thick - an appropriate phrase if I've ever heard one.

As Clive looked on, I explained what would now happen. If nothing still occurred, the good old snatch squads would come into the stand and indiscriminately pluck people from the crowd in an effort to rile us. And so it was. What do you mean waste of tax payers money, and hopefully Wigan's tax payers money? At the end of the game with the "Mexican stand-off" still in place, they allow hundreds of Wigan on to the pitch unimpeded by stewards or police and permit them to taunt and abuse us for several minutes from behind the safety of the police lines. Brave show lads!

Outside the ground the police formed an impenetrable barrier and blocked our route to cars, coaches and any trains. They again indiscriminately pushed, shoved and attempted to intimidate us into a response, including forcing some people, women and children included, down a slope that ran into a stream running alongside. They then decided to drive us back away from our route by running police horses through us in both directions, including the way they'd told us to go. This a mere couple of weeks after a fan was trampled to death at Rotherham. Bricks and abuse were thrown, they videoed the whole shebang, which I'm sure will not be edited in any way.

Once in the car park, we were forced to stand in the pouring rain for no apparent reason and then had to almost give the police a bill of sale to prove we actually had a van. Clive and I attempt to find Simon and Patrick who we'd lost in the melee and were pushed and threatened by the nearest officer for our trouble. We attempted to discover exactly which tactical genius had decided the night's policy and were basically told it was only us that caused trouble and it was all on video. Naturally it was, and in all its unexpurgated glory I'm sure. Strangely, I thought Stoke's fans had rioted at Wigan and I thought Wigan themselves were also mentioned as being involved in half a dozen other incidents. Perhaps I'm mistaken.

If the police were honest, they know that the "all dressed up with nothing to do – we're harder than you" attitude is the reality on nights like this. It gives them a chance to open their boxes of tricks and use them against us. Arm yourself to the teeth and of course you're harder than us. You're dressed up like a medieval knight, abuse your privileges willy nilly, and have the full weight of the law to back up anything you do. Of course you're harder than us, but only for this reason.

CHAPTER 19

A GRAND DAY OUT

SOME GAMES STAND out in your mind, even amongst so many away trips. I've listed a few for your delectation.

READING - THAMES VALLEY ROYALS: For some reason Reading away always throws up something, so in no particular order:-

The spanner throwing, Uwe Fuchs debut (Millwall fans will understand), Dave's wank offer, a two hour delayed train trip, our shunt with Mr Moody at a fancy dressed "pissed as old Harry" New Year's Day game, Simon getting hit on the head with a rock thrown by a Millwall fan at the Madejski in 1999, a game at which Paul's car also broke down.

But for sheer action packed drama, nothing compares to our clash on the 30th of April, 1983. Steve K and I travelled to the most eventful game I've ever seen, home or away. At this time, that awfully nice Robert Maxwell was trying to merge Reading and Oxford to form the exotically named Thames Valley Royals. This prompted both sets of fans to go "overboard" – no pun intended – and arrange demonstrations against it.

During the hours prior to this relegation struggle, the home fans had marched through town in protest at this deeply unpopular move. The chanting and banner waving continued in the ground and during the match. At this time Reading were fourth from bottom and Millwall third from bottom of the old Division Three, with us one point behind and with a game in hand.

The programme for this game was oblong, i.e. not very deep, but wide. My copy also has two front covers, so if any programme collector wants to give me £50, he can have it! It claimed to have been voted best programme of Division Three in 1981 / 1982 by commercial managers. Now if this is an example of excellence in their judgement, I can only assume that they must drink more than licensed Victuallers.

This game at Elm Park kicked off in a highly volatile atmosphere. Millwall proceeded to leak goals in Cavalier gay abandon style. This prompted a couple of pitch invasions from the away end. The first half ended 3-1 and with two men sent off, Ian Stewart and Dean Neal. Millwall staged the greatest comeback since Lazarus and

133

pulled it back to 3-3. As Millwall also had a penalty, I think you can call it quite an eventful day. I think to call the end of game celebrations wild would not be an overstatement. A full day's fun and no mistakes, more action than *Escape To Victory* – mind you, that's not hard come to think of it.

CHESTERFIELD - THE ABYSS: After this game we could have done the unthinkable, in my lifetime, and slipped into the bottomless pit that is Division Three (Four). This was the last game of 1982/3 season under George Graham. Steve K and I drove up on the 14th of May, 1983, to Derbyshire. We saw a crooked spire, our windscreen wiper fell off, we convinced a doubting landlord, and praise the Lord! We won 1-0 with a Dave Cusack penalty. I couldn't get a programme. This upsets me as I have a ritual of throwing them unread into the cupboard. Don't ask me why. We started this game behind the goal on an open terrace. It started to monsoon, so we ran to the side covered sheds. In my inimitable fashion, I fell over and cut my hand open. We took the ground over, wrecked some seats and ran into the home end. Chesterfield were already down, we occupied 90% of the ground and we stayed up.

BOURNEMOUTH - POPPING THE CHERRY: In our promotion season, our penultimate game away in old Division Two was a night match at Bournemouth, a game shown on a big screen at The Old Den. Colin and I managed to get tickets in the Bournemouth seats to witness another dramatic night, a 2-1 win including a Terry Hurlock screamer and a late Brian Horne penalty save. We were beginning to think the unthinkable, i.e. promotion up to the Big Boys and this game was a cornerstone in my book. It was odd sitting in seats with "posh" people. I felt like continually tugging my forelock in supplication, because I'm just a commoner. A blinding night, you had to be there.

HULL CITY - WHAT D'YA MEAN, WE'RE CHAMPIONS?: We travelled up to Hull on a special direct to the station beside Hull's ground. I'd started out on my own for this Championship clincher in May 1988, but I met a few blokes I knew at the station and travelled up with them. We decided to play cards, Pontoon, I was mostly the banker, with a capital W in my case, as I managed to skint myself to the tune of £40. Contrary to popular practices, I'm not sure of the actual figure, as I stopped counting when my eyes glazed over with tears.

I remember stopping at Doncaster station. The train was packed with Millwall, with flags and scarves decorating the windows as we pulled into the station. The look of abject terror on the platform's inhabitants was a picture, a cross between "Any last requests?" and "Why me, God?" Cue audible sigh of collective relief as we pulled out again. It's strange what reaction you get when a media induced pre-conception becomes an in-your-face reality, isn't it?

We passed the Humber Bridge, and bloody impressive it is too. We pulled into the station at Hull and were greeted like conquering heroes by the Millwall already there. We had about 6,000 up there that day. The game wasn't much, as I recall, but we won 1-0 with an O'Callaghan penalty, the second in two consecutive away matches. He scored at Bournemouth as well – unheard of. It was announced at full-time, we were champions. Champions? It didn't sink in to me, even though there was a mass conga in full swing on the pitch and much player hoisting. I came back on the train in a bit of a daze. Champions?

For some reason – financial mostly! – I didn't want to play cards on the way home. As soon as I got home one of my mates, Steve, who's a Tottenham fan, called and had to drag me to the pub. As you can imagine, I had half a shandy and a drambuie chaser and went home early. If you believe that I must sell you my time share ideas. Give me a call.

I returned the compliment after Spurs won the FA Cup, visiting a pub in Tottenham High Street, amidst mass jubilation. I'd just got back from our 4-1 play-off coshing at Brighton and stood in this pub, mumbling and sobbing into my beer decked out in my Millwall shirt, much to the locals' bemusement. I needed a drink for shock and hired a St Bernard brandy dog for the night just in case.

I celebrated our Championship success after the Blackburn game by going in my local, The Old Rose, on the Highway. The governor, Barry, is another Millwall fan, so me and another old mate, Ian, went down there. My companions from the Hull trip were there. I graciously turned down their card school invitation and we got stuck into the light ales and singing any Millwall song we knew. There were a few other East End Millwall as well. We draped a large Millwall Union Jack on the DJ's decks and played *Let 'Em Come* and *The Ballad Of Harry Cripps* all night. We enjoyed ourselves. I wouldn't necessarily say that the non-football regulars did, but once in a hundred years has got to be celebrated, wouldn't you agree? And I did celebrate, don't you worry.

LIVERPOOL - HEART ATTACK? DIE HAPPY: In the top flight, as they say, we'd played a lot of away matches prior to this, but for me walking out on the away terrace at Anfield meant we'd arrived. We honestly were in Division One! The atmosphere was electric, we had about 4,000 fans crammed in the corner of a stand facing The Kop, we all sang our heads off all afternoon, out singing and generally taking the piss out of our illustrious hosts. They certainly knew we were there, that's for sure. Miraculously we took the lead and also hit a post for good measure. When we scored I nearly had a shock induced coronary.

"How is he Doctor?"

"Heart attack. He's dead I'm afraid."

"Really? Why's he grinning like a lunatic then?"

This game surpassed all my expectations. Talking to non-Millwall mates prior to this game, cricket scores and early Liverpool declarations were mooted as the likely outcome, but here we were leading at Anfield!

Sadly it didn't last and the game finished 1-1. Liverpool played well, but had "Home Town Harry" as a ref. Who did permit them to kick lumps out of us at any opportunity and go unpunished? For me this was the day. If you watched the game only on the big screen at The Den, I feel sorry for you, because as that Welsh prat, Max Boyce, would say, "I was there!"

The fun didn't end there, though. We serenaded the stragglers in the ground who had to just stand and take it. We left the ground and noticed that the Merseyside Police didn't seem overly friendly for some reason. They also seemed to be equipped with whopping great "billy" sticks, more like those used by police on horseback in London. For both Merseyside clubs, Liverpool and Everton, the policy was to load the away fans on to double decker buses and ferry you back to Edge Hill station to get the specials home. They used the same tactic on the way to the ground when the special trains were convoyed en masse to Anfield via the more recession hit areas of the city. This led to much "Loadsamoney" style wad waving. This, as you can imagine, elicited a less than cheery response from the locals. I remember in one case a 10 year old boy, obviously Britain's youngest subscriber to the Red Hot And Dutch porn channel, who gave us his best Linda Lovelace blow job impression. Don't kids grow up younger these days?!

At this game I didn't see any trouble personally, unlike the first visit to Everton, a return visit that followed a Cup game in the early 70s where several Millwall fans were stabbed. Here we saw pubs emptying out to greet us, skirmishes with stragglers in the street, trouble with police horses blocking our exit to assist these individuals outside the ground, and a cherry bomb thrown at the bus I was on.

For the Liverpool match we arrived back at Edge Hill, unmolested, mob handed. The jolly Scouse constabulary then adopted what came to be the normal strategy for later visits. That was to line everyone up outside the station and make us wait for the train, usually a long wait. I've had this happen elsewhere and it always struck me as an odd ploy. I'd have thought you'd have a train or trains waiting upon arrival in order to get the away fans out of your jurisdiction as quickly as possible, but what do I know?

At this game I think the police were a little miffed that we'd had the audacity to come here and not meekly allow ourselves to get soundly thrashed. They marched up and down our ranks, Gestapo like, waiting for any excuse to drag any dissenters out and give them a more "hands-on" version of the local hospitality. Someone in the crowd started singing "Strolling, just strolling", that strange song about shagging ponies, at least I think that's the words, to accompany the singing, which was now communal. We swayed rhythmically from side to side, as this seemed to aggravate the local Old Bill even more.

We naturally continued, expanding our repertoire with *Maybe It's Because I'm A Londoner*, *My Old Man's A Dustman*, and any other chirpy Cockney favourites we could think of, all accompanied with swaying. It's a pity Tommy Steele or Stanley Holloway weren't there or we could have burst into a full musical style knees-up. Now that would have been funny.

In the event the police took this as a sleight on their "Scousehood", but it certainly jollied us through our wait, I can tell you. So much for that great Scouse sense of humour. It could have deteriorated. I suppose they could have fought back with Jimmy Tarbuck, Cilla Black or the ultimate deterrent - Stan Boardman, and his hilarious skits on Germans bombing his chip shop. I think the trains arrived in time to avoid this terrible weapon being unleashed.

The five away games I've mentioned are ones that stick in my mind probably more than any others. One good one at home came in 1998/1999 against Blackpool, when my mate Simon had his son Patrick as the club mascot. Daughter Lisa was also invited to take part. The club gave the kids the chance to meet the players, have club shirts signed, have their picture taken, warm-up with the players, lead the team out and have a pre-match kickabout. Patrick also got his picture in the programme and his name on the scoreboard.

The kids took all of this quite calmly. Simon, on the other hand, was like a "dog with two dicks" or the "cat that got the cream", if you prefer a cleaner analogy. He had a pre-match kick about in front of the South Stand (C.B.L.) where we're all season ticket holders. Naturally being friends we lampooned his footballing skills and pointed out that having seen his talents, he wasn't in a position to complain about anyone ever again. Afterwards we all met up with Simon babbling excitedly and Pat and Lisa quite blasé about it all. True fans would be the same, I know I would. As a postscript, Pat goes to most of the away matches, Lisa too, but less often. He's been to 25 or so grounds already at 8 years old, so there's no hope for him at all, I'm sorry to say.

CHAPTER 20

THE (SHEEP) LOVER'S GUIDE

ON MY TRAVELS I've had the pleasure of visiting many rural type clubs in the English and Welsh countryside, a few I've already mentioned - Plymouth, Lincoln and Wycombe - in other chapters and I haven't mentioned Cardiff, Swansea or Bristol City again, as these are much less like a jolly country jaunt and more like a trip to the Wild West. Not exactly all quiet on the Western Front, the attitude being "Get orf my land". So on a more (mainly) peaceful tip . . .

WESTWARD HO!

WREXHAM: I've only been to Wrexham once in October, 1998. At this particular time the weather was appalling with most rivers, particularly in the west, on flood alert. Myself, Simon, Patrick, Nathan, and Paul set off on the club coach from The New Den with a certain amount of trepidation and expectations of the radio announcing that the match was off. We headed up the motorway north-westwards and stopped off for lunch at a lorry driver's truck stop somewhere near Shrewsbury. It had been raining all day, which only added to our assumption that it would be cancelled at any minute. At the truck stop we queued up to order our nosh.

Unlike the motorway services, the food we got was of "Desperate Dan" cow pie proportions and certainly added a bit of ballast for our very damp trip. We crossed over into Wales almost without noticing we'd left England. I thought it was a bit strange, it was my first ever trip to Wales and I was expecting close harmony singing, road signs that looked like a bad hand of scrabble, coal miners, and nervous looking sheep amid rolling, welcoming hillsides, but to be honest it looked exactly like Shropshire and the locals sounded more like Scousers than the "Look you, boyo" type of dialect I was expecting.

Nowhere like as alien as South Wales to my mind, anyway. As we drove towards the ground we passed through water lapping at the side of the road, with the rivers almost bursting their banks and flooding across the road in many places. We carried on with the local radio on, and to be honest, reached the ground in heavy rain, fully expecting to find out it was off, even as late as going through the turnstiles. But no.

In the confusion, Simon took Patrick on to the terrace not having noticed that Paul, Nathan and myself had headed to the seats. The ground was a bit strange, with one side of The Racecourse Ground looking derelict with an old pub stuck in one corner. The rest of the ground was adequate enough and the game started, damp but on an amazingly good pitch all things considered.

The game was awful, ended 0-0, Ian Rush came on for a brief stint and the band of the Grenadier Guards serenaded us. Something to do with drumming up support for the Remembrance Day charity. We left and headed back to London only to hit a flooded underpass just outside London and had the pleasure of sitting in a massive traffic jam for what seemed like an eternity. Splendid!

SWINDON: Apparently Melinda Messenger, Billie Piper, and Julian Clary come from Swindon. I don't quite know what that says about the place, but I thought I'd mention it.

I've been to Swindon on several occasions and always seem to have to sit or stand in a different part of the ground. I've sat behind one goal, stood in the corner of the other end and sat high up one end of a stand on two other occasions. During the 1994 / 1995 season, under Mick McCarthy, we played at Swindon twice. On our League visit we won quite comfortably, so assumed that our League Cup Quarter Final visit would be an easy stroll. We drove there in Dave's car, myself, Paul and Simon. We got there very early, joined the other Millwall encamped in McDonalds, and went back to our car to get out of the biting January winds.

In a great Millwall tradition we blew it and lost, a defeat that included a massive fluke or superb goal by Fjortoft, which flew into the net past a bewildered keeper and prompted Mick McCarthy to say something like "If he meant that, I'll bare my arse in Burton's window."

Dear old Mick was Oscar Wilde-like in his pronouncements, another classic being, "I hope his next shit's a hedgehog," after a dubious decision by a linesman. I hope the officials carry industrial strength anusol should this eventually arise! I saw Mick McCarthy at Charing Cross station when he was still Millwall's manager, looking like a colour blind test, dressed in oranges and greens in true "I got dressed in the dark" colour co-ordination mode.

BRISTOL ROVERS: I've never seen Millwall win at any of Bristol Rovers' grounds, in fact in some half a dozen trips we've only picked up one point - on my first visit to Eastville. I've been by train, coach, car and National Express bus once via Bath for a bit of culture. As I'd rather not talk about the games, I'll mention the grounds instead.

Eastville: Lovely, just like a run down White City with rusty old sheds, a dog track, and with a motorway flyover not far above your head.

Twerton: Well indescribable, more Shaw Taylor than Taylor Report, i.e. criminal. A real amateur ground in all senses, it was getting gradually better prior to the move back to Bristol. The only thing to recommend a trip to Twerton was that you got to see Bath, which really is a nice place. Nothing else.

One strange thing they used to do at Twerton was to have a roving microphone man who shoved a mike in some poor unsuspecting kid's face and asked him to predict the final score. The kid usually predicted a cakewalk for whichever side he supported. He took a bit of a risk with this odd idea I thought, particularly in our section, but that's showbiz I suppose.

Memorial Ground: Keeping up a proud tradition, this is a real hotch potch with a tent at one end, a small shed at the other, a stand opposite the away terrace that looks like they've nicked it from a racecourse, and finally a stand that is moveable. We spoke to a steward before our Boxing Day trip in 1999 and he said that they're going to move this stand backwards into the park behind and build a new ground the other way around to its current position, with this side stand now being behind the goal. Good luck.

OXFORD: The ground's not in Oxford, but a few miles outside in Headington, not too flash and never shown on Inspector Morse as part of Oxford's dreaming spires. A partner in Robert Maxwell's fiendish plan to merge with Reading to form one mighty Thames Valley club, the current ground is one of the "We've got a few quid, let's build something new which bares no relationship to anything else in the ground" type of jobs prevalent in the lower divisions. I've been here many times, I've listed the various ways in other chapters, but I'm really looking forward to going to their new ground which I believe is being built in a cesspit or next to a fertiliser factory or something. Just hope you get a game away from the summer, as it would be particularly pungent then. Maybe Oxford could get some club coloured clothes pegs or gas masks for the occasion.

NOT QUITE UP NORTH

NORTHAMPTON: A ground I've only been to in the recent past, a nice new ground in the mode of Wycombe, Scunthorpe and Walsall, this one is in a small valley with a lot of shops, restaurants, bars, etc., and a proper car park. We usually do quite well here, but lost on my first visit when the ref moved in mysterious ways in his decision making. The last time we went there we drove up, arrived fairly early and went in search of food - McDonalds in our case as Patrick <u>must</u> have only McDonalds.

This meant in this instance walking past Burger King and making a bee-line for his favourite burger shop, which was a bit of a trek away. We did say that he couldn't really tell the difference and would have a job telling one from the other if we blindfolded him, but no go. He's had the pleasure of a Big Mac in Watford, Fulham, Colchester, Notts County, Northampton, Gillingham and anywhere else we pass one. Simon even tracked one down in Barcelona when they did a tour of the Nou Camp stadium whilst on holiday.

Also at Northampton they have their own version of what we used to call Jews Hill at The Old Den, where the freeloaders would gather behind the goal. At Northampton it's on a grass verge that looks towards the away fans. Cheapskate cobblers!

EASTWARD YO!

CAMBRIDGE: A place of many bicycles, studious looking types and scholarly people in Tom Baker Dr Who style scarves. The ground is a real treat with a stream running up one side. I've been there a few times, seen a win, draw and a loss, so there you are. The away end consists of about six steps, with the back row behind the goal bringing your eyeline in direct line with the crossbar. We usually drive there as it's a local game. I went once on the train. This way brings you through the bike shed section of town.

I've had my picture featured in Millwall's programme showing my mug resplendent on the magnificent away terrace at the palatial Abbey Stadium.

One recentish game I missed was our 1-0 giant killing exit of a few years ago when due to my psychic ability, I knew we'd get beat and we did by an apparently brilliantly executed own goal by David Thompson in the pissing down of rain. So I think my absence was the right choice.

COLCHESTER: The ground at Colchester is real "Beazer Homes pre-fab League Division Four" stuff. The away "shed" is the most claustrophobic stand I've ever been in, with only one toilet for the thousand or so of us, hopefully non-incontinent fans. The area around the ground is in the residential part of the town, the home fans consist of squaddy types and "almost" Cockneys. I've been twice, seen one draw and one win. We had a wander around the oldie worldie town and walked the many miles, or so it seemed, from the station the last time we went by train, me, Simon and Patrick. The other time we drove there as it's another short little jaunt for us. The only notable thing I can recall apart from our glorious victory on my last visit was that after this game we had a wait for the train, so we wandered off to the chip shop and whilst eating my pie and chips I managed to spill it all down my nice white shirt. You can't take me anywhere.

BOOTIFUL!

NORWICH CITY: I like Norwich as a city, it's a place I've been to on many occasions, mostly when on holiday in Great Yarmouth. We would take a day trip to see the street market and castle, etc. My first football visit was in the late 60s when my Mum and Dad took me to see Norwich play Blackpool, a true explosion in a paint factory job, yellow, green and tangerine. No floodlights needed for these games I can tell you. Not usually a place for trouble, in fact the only Norwich related trouble I've ever seen was at Yarmouth when a mob of Norwich skinheads rampaged along the promenade in the 60s to do battle with the rockers on their motorbikes, pulling them off their bikes and throwing missiles etc. Made me feel right at home for some reason.

It was at Norwich that Micky and I first met Jim Stephenson and Dave Murray in a pub on the riverside, two more of my frequent companions home and away since. I've only seen Millwall twice at Carrow Road, once for a draw in the old First Division relegation season and once for a rearranged FA Cup tie in February, 1992, a game we lost 2-1, missed a penalty and had about 4,000 fans crammed in the section of terracing and seats next to the home fans section with a roof to floor fence between us. This was one of the loudest away crowd performances I've ever heard, so we did our bit anyway. It's always interesting home or away against Norwich with a League Cup quarter final game at The Old Den during the three day weeks in December, 1973, and a 3-2 defeat at The Old Den in

143

the old First Division (one of the best ever live TV games) being highlights. A tip for any turkeys reading this - you're not safe in Norfolk!

IPSWICH TOWN: Like Norwich, a good ground for atmosphere before all-seater grounds. The away fans were penned in next to the home fans behind the goal, again with a roof to floor fence. The usual taunts from us are agriculture related accompanied with sheep noises, etc. Our best performance was a 3-0 win in the early Nineties when we also had the privilege of giving Ipswich sub, Paul Goddard, a through barracking in the season after his dismal showings for us and also for previously playing for West Ham.

On the trips I've been by train we've gone into the nearest pub to the station and found it totally occupied by Lions. Suits me. Of my visits, the most memorable for all the wrong reasons was our vital relegation battle on the 5th of May, 1996. We went by coach, me, Simon and Clive. We headed off from The New Den, through "A" roads etc, getting stuck in country lanes and being held up by a car boot sale somewhere in Essex.

At the game we took over one side stand and watched a tortuous 0-0 game which saw us relegated to Division Two. I managed to bruise my hands by rhythmically thumping the surrounding wall, which I sat behind as an accompaniment to our trying to roar the Lions to victory. The good old Millwall jungle telegraph was also in full swing with fictitious tales of favourable results coming through. Simon had his Walkman on, so knew that Portsmouth, our only possible saviours, weren't losing at all. At the end, trouble broke out, as you might expect, and we headed back to London, disembarked at Aldgate and headed back to Whitechapel.

We met some fellow Lions there who'd had the pleasure of West Ham's welcoming committee on their return trip to Liverpool Street station. They said it was like walking into a scene from an old prison film with the Hammers massed on the walkways above the concourse. We missed this personally, but I did get one car load of blokes taunting me for my team getting relegated. Thanks for mentioning it. I hadn't noticed.

In 2000 we played at Ipswich in a Second Round second leg Worthington Cup game. We led 2-0 from the first leg and set off in good spirits in the minibus with the usual suspects. The game itself was like nothing I've ever seen before.

Millwall's main forward, Neil Harris, went off injured early on, so we brought on a 17 year old to play up front on his own against a

144

Premiership defence. We had a man sent off for two bookable offences (in the ref's opinion anyway), one of which conceded a penalty, but our keeper saved it. Millwall then took off another forward to bring on a defender to replace the one sent off, and we somehow held out until half-time.

In the second half it was nothing short of The Alamo. Ipswich must have put in about 50 crosses and Millwall's defence did a rearguard action of Dunkirk proportions. It looked like we'd survive, so the ref decided to make it easier for the home side by sending off another Millwall player. Within minutes, Ipswich scored (by now the 78th minute) and the siege resumed. With the two man advantage, the Ipswich crossing bombardment continued. We thought we'd make it, but in the 88th minute, Ipswich scored a goal which looked suspiciously like handball. The radio said so and so did Sky, so there. They also said that the penalty was a dive. Conspiracy theorist, who me?

The ref's performance was enhanced further in extra time when we had two players off the field injured, effectively leaving Millwall with seven players against Ipswich's full team. He forced one of the injured players back on to the pitch so that he could legally continue. We lost 5-0 in the end, but I've never seen such stoic resistance. We even had the cheek to almost sneak a goal prior to extra time. If we had scored, I'd have asked Mad Ted to marry me in all the excitement.

We drove home down hearted and worn out. We'd had to stand up the whole game, and quite honestly I'm not used to it anymore. The support from our fans all night had been ear splitting and continuous so we'd all done our bit. Dave, who was driving the mini-bus, dropped us off in Chingford where his son Paul's car was waiting to take us back to the East End. As there were six of us and only five seats, Nathan volunteered to travel in the boot - a surreal end to a surreal day! If we'd been stopped it would have looked like an Eastern European human smuggling ring!

One thing that I forgot to mention is that on our way up we passed a field of sheep painted with red dayglo paint at the rear end. I assume to aid the shepherd on his nocturnal love quests. Best not to think about it!

SOUL BOY RACERS IN THE BADLANDS

SOUTHEND: Land of short skirts, boob tubes and stilettos, and that's only the men, boom boom! In the 60s/70s Southend used to be the destination for East End skinhead invasions on Bank Holidays, when a large contingent from East London would gather at Stepney East station and get the train to the seaside only to be met by the police who confiscated their laces and braces. Spoilsports.

Another place I've been to about eight times. Again, like Swindon, I've been on every side of the ground as the home team switched the away section about. Usually another invasion ground as it's a "local" derby. We usually drive ourselves or go by train to Prittlewell, home of Barry Fry, Stan Collymore, ex-pat Cockneys, "Kiss Me Quick" hats and winkle stalls.

Again we usually do well with a few memorable moments, namely Steve K and my "gay bar" mistake, a 3-3 Sunday televised match, the venue of Terry Hurlock's second coming, the day the away horde turned on Mick McCarthy when he announced his interest in leaving to manage the Republic Of Ireland and was serenaded with "Fuck off Mick McCarthy!" etc., and a return visit by the prolific Millwall scorer, Teddy Sheringham, who whilst sitting in the stand for one of our games in the 90s was given a standing ovation.

However, the most notorious game was an FA Cup game at Roots Hall in midweek in the early Nineties, when Stan Collymore was in a mood he usually reserved for Ulrika, and in a 1-0 defeat, managed to wind our crowd up with his antics. Our hostile reaction thus gave Essex's finest the chance to bring out the riot armoury and adopt the snatch squad tactic. This led to seat throwing and a sweet shop being ransacked. Volatile, but not too bad in reality. Some shops were attacked, so not too good if you were some poor sod who ran one of these, I suppose. I used to do a lot of work for a company near the ground in Southend and was told of Leicester fans trying to burn down the ten pin bowling alley and Derby's pitch invasion in the early 90s. Must be something in the old sea air.

CHAPTER 21

WHERE WERE YOU AT MACCLESFIELD?

WEMBLEY, APRIL 1999. I never thought I'd live to see the day. It's a pity that it wasn't the League or FA Cup final or even a play-off final, but what the hell. I was determined to enjoy the day come what may, even though Millwall, in time honoured fashion, lost to a very dodgy, very late losing goal. It didn't really matter, it wasn't the Auto Windscreen Trophy that was important. I've been a Millwall fan long enough to expect this as the likely outcome, but I'd fulfilled my dream – I'd seen us at Wembley.

Typical Millwall luck. We win the inaugural League Trophy, a forerunner of this trophy, at Lincoln, when a few years later it becomes a Wembley day out. We came third in Division Two in 1972 when the season after three up became the norm. We'd have the better goal difference the very season that goals scored was the norm and vice versa. Bad luck or a conspiracy? Being paranoid, the latter obviously.

The build up to the game had been fantastic post Regional Final win. Grown men like us were pleading with local newsagents for our Neil Harris *Evening Standard* posters, all a bit of a worry actually. Sad but true. The phrases "Woodwork" and "Coming out of" spring to mind. I'd always dreamt that a final with Millwall would break all previous volume records at Wembley. My equation went: usual Millwall volume multiplied by additional 30,000 fans equals one hell of a racket.

One snag to this I'm afraid. Sadly most of those present weren't what I'd call real Millwall, not week-in – week-out, come rain or shine people like us, and didn't know half the songs, largely because most of them fell into one of these categories: glory hunting bandwagon jumper, fair weather Charlies who'd probably not set foot in The New Den - and probably hadn't gone at all since we got relegated from the top flight, they'd not been since Harry Cripps last played, they had not actually ever seen a Millwall game in the flesh, or supported some other team and only attended with Millwall mates.

Our own party probably highlighted the likely make up of the crowd. It consisted of me, Simon, Patrick, Lisa, Dave, Paul, Nathan,

Mad Ted and Clive, regulars at home and for most of us 15 – 20 away games a seasoners as well. In addition my old friend, Colin, from Dorset a lifetime fan who didn't go very often any more due to distance and family commitments, another mate Danny who occasionally goes, some friends of friends, my mate JB who supports Spurs but has Millwall family connections, a few lapsed or very lapsed Lions fans, Simon's mate, Tony, and Little Tony, who supported Arsenal, but who wanted to take his son to Wembley before they knocked it down and had had trouble getting Arsenal European tickets. That was our lot – 28 in all and fairly typical, I'd say.

I volunteered to get everyone's tickets, because that's the sort of chap I am. I got to The Den at about 9.00am armed with a fist full of "oncers" and umpteen season tickets, Junior Lions and membership cards. On arrival I was just a smidge cheesed off to find that we regular home and away-ers were put on an equal footing with members, who irrespective of length of membership (they could have joined up the day before), could get tickets exactly as we could. Quite how we didn't get privileges over these "Johnny come lately, don't go at all's" I don't know. How this was a fair system is beyond me. If for some reason I'd not got my rightful quota of tickets due to this policy decision, I'd have been "ropeable".

A few observations on "The Day Of The Long Queue". Firstly, it was bloody hot and my full length leather jacket wasn't a good idea. Secondly, the general conversation highlighted my preconceptions about the "woodwork" faction.

"I usually go shopping with the wife Saturday . . . "

"I always go fishing weekends . . . "

Both ending with ". . . but you've got to go to this one."

Why?

This line of conversation seemed to be quite prevalent. The many regulars who I knew from either home or away greeted each other like a secret society, with imperceptive nods and gestures indicating a kind of fellowship amongst all these strangers. Thirdly the queue also exhibited that great Millwall talent for wild speculation and unfounded rumour. "They've sold 60,000 tickets, there's only the Royal Box left!" sort of tosh.

This spreads like wildfire and implausible, not to say ridiculous or not, it burrows into your brain, until you're convinced that the very moment you get to the window, the "Sorry, sold out" signs will shoot up. The doubts are only erased when you've physically got your tickets in your grubby mitts.

148

The "woodwork" people reminded me of a story I heard about a Gillingham v. Everton game in the Cup several years ago. Steve K had a friend whose wife worked in the Gillingham ticket office. For this popular game she told of one bloke who called up to get tickets, had a lengthy conversation about his lifetime's devotion and spoiled it all by asking where the ground actually was. To my mind, you either support a team or you don't. By support I mean going home and away as often as is physically and financially possible, sick notes from your mum excepted, come rain, shine, wind or snow, and irrespective of opposition or club predicament.

I can't personally understand why some people feel a sudden urge to turn up for the "Bertie Big Bollocks" games and show no inclination whatsoever to go to the more mundane fixtures against normal opposition. I couldn't give a monkey's who we're playing, because I'm going to watch Millwall and not the opponents, who could be Real Madrid or Rochdale for all I care.

I got the tickets and distributed them far and wide and we made travel plans for the day. The game coincided with the London Marathon. Unfortunately, or otherwise, I live in Docklands, which means on Marathon days I'm penned in on all sides by running pantomime cows, men dressed as women (nothing unusual there), idiots juggling and all manner of strange sights. The only means of escape is to leave home at the cock's crow or wait until late afternoon or catch a DLR train to the next stop up the line, where I can then cross the road. Strange but true.

Colin came up the night before and stayed at my place overnight. We met up with Danny at Shadwell DLR and walked up to Aldgate station where we met up with a lot of the East End contingent including Micky, Steve and brood, and all my usual mates. Anyone who came from outside London was to make their own way for gather-up later at the ground. Luckily the line to Wembley Park starts at Aldgate, so we had the luxury of a seat on an initially empty train. By the time we arrived at Wembley the train was packed mostly with strangers. The regulars again exchanged secret society nods in recognition and we left the station.

Coming on to Wembley Way was fantastic – a sea of blue and white, Millwall flags, shirts, badges, scarves, etc. The two paths up to Wembley itself were signposted "Wigan" and "Millwall". The left hand side "Wigan" path consisted of one man and his whippet, the wind howling and old Wild West tumbleweeds blowing along its empty road. By comparison we were crammed in sardine like as a human river of Lions made their way to the ground.

Inside the ground the concourses were packed and the atmosphere was like I'd hoped with Millwall songs bouncing off the walls. It was excellent, very noisy. Inside the stadium proper the sight of tens of thousands of blue and white balloons and Millwall flags was awesome. Throughout the game – no classic sadly – the volume of the singing was disappointing. I'd anticipated tinnitus levels of volume and was actually able to hear myself think, which given my mind is no bonus.

In the ground we were at the end Wigan "scored" and were within waving distance of my Uncle Peter and cousins Paul and Gavin, long time home and away-ers like myself. Must run in the family. We waved at each other across the blocks in recognition of a familiar face. We usually see each other at home and away games. We don't travel together, as they live in Chelmsford.

The game drifted by, genuine penalties turned down, dodgy goal given. We left. Outside we hung about to let the crowds clear, we got some food and bumped into Barry Kitchener and his wife, a really nice bloke. It's a funny feeling when you meet a boyhood hero in the flesh. I now know how Simon felt at his kid's mascot game.

We walked back to Wembley Central, got a train to Euston and I said "Why don't you come to my flat in Docklands?" Most agreed and we made the trek east. Picture the scene – Millwall flags, shirts and the kids blue-painted faces, turning up on a "posh" marina, where except for me, the token Cockney, the inhabitants are all jolly well to do. Imagine the spluttering in their Pimms and falling off their yachts in shock that our appearance provoked. I was expecting a strong letter from the tenants association and Yacht Club for lowering the tone. We went into a pub on the river that had a DJ, band and numerous tight whitet-shirted barmaids. It was national "Breast Awareness" day or something and we were all certainly aware, I can tell you.

It was a great day all in all, despite my moaning previously. Don't mind me, I'm Millwall, it's in my job description to whinge. Sorry.

WE FEAR NO FOE
A Decade Of Following Millwall

Colin Johnson is a casually dressed white male in his late twenties. He is not a "football hooligan", just a loyal fan who follows his team home and away. His team is Millwall. We Fear No Foe! is his story of following the Lions over the last decade despite the nonsense Millwall fans have to face week in week out from the police, rival fans, the media, the authorities, and even their own club from time to time. Not that all Millwall fans are angels either . . .   Price £8.99

ST GEORGE IN MY HEART
Confessions Of An England Fan

When he's not on domestic duty with Millwall, Colin Johnson spends his time and money following his beloved England over land and sea. And not as part of the official travel club either. Here's his account of trips to Scotland, Italy, Ireland, Wales, Poland, Czechoslovakia, Sweden, Spain, Holland, and of course Wembley before it became populated by happy smiley people chanting "Football's coming home".   Price £8.99

INVASION AND DEPORTATION
A Diary Of Euro 2000

Darlo fan, Jamie Mash, and his Arsenal following cousin, Matthew Bazell, are two England fans whose dreams of following England to European glory via the qualifying games and the finals turned into a nightmare of being arrested and deported in Belgium (or in Jamie's case, France, but that's another story). Forget the tabloid headlines and the 20 second TV footage. Here's what it's really like to follow England abroad.   Price £8.99

The above books are available from all good bookshops or by post from STP MAIL ORDER, P.O. Box 12, Lockerbie. DG11 3BW. Make cheques payable to STP Mail Order. There is nothing to add for postage and packing. We send books and CDs all over the world.

Also from Terrace Banter

BRING OUT YOUR RIOT GEAR - Hearts Are Here!

Welcome to an Edinburgh that doesn't exist in the tourist guides. An Edinburgh where youths fought each other over territory, style and football. During the Eighties, Edinburgh's underbelly became a battlefield for mods, punks, skinheads and casuals. And as Hearts struggled on the pitch, it was their hooligan following that was making all the news. Towns and cities all over Scotland knew the meaning of Gorgie Aggro. It was the excitement of being part of an invading hooligan army that attracted C.S. Ferguson and his friends to Hearts, first as a young gang mod and then as one of the first recruits to the infamous Casual Soccer Firm. Here's his story. Bring Out Your Riot Gear - Hearts Are Here! Also includes an extract from Gavin Anderson's Fighting For The Red, White And Blue.   Price £8.99

SINGIN' THE BLUES - CARLISLE UNITED

Singin' The Blues is the story of author Neil Nixon and his undying love for Carlisle United. Covering thirty years of triumph and tragedy the book records the passions and nightmares that have kept alive the longest lasting love affair of the author's life. Broken into chapters dedicated to his famous and infamous footballing heroes, the story rotates humour, honest accounts of grim struggles and those sweet but occasional moments of victory.
A book for anyone who has ever cared about the also rans of the sporting world and one that shows the uninitiated why they should care.   Price £9.99

The above books are available from all good bookshops or by post from STP MAIL ORDER, P.O. Box 12, Lockerbie. DG11 3BW. Make cheques payable to STP Mail Order. There is nothing to add for postage and packing. We send books and CDs all over the world.

**We are always interested in hearing from authors and potential authors who would like to see their football book published by Terrace Banter. You can write to us at:
Terrace Banter, ST Publishing, PO Box 12, Lockerbie, Dumfriesshire. DG11 3BW.**

**www.terracebanter.com
info@terracebanter.com**